TARAWA

The Incredible Story of One of World War II's Bloodiest Battles

ROBERT SHERROD

Skyhorse Publishing

Skyhorse Publishing books may be purchased in bulk at special discounts for sales promotion, corporate gifts, fund-raising, or educational purposes. Special editions can also be created to specifications. For details, contact the Special Sales Department, Skyhorse Publishing, 307 West 36th Street, 11th Floor, New York, NY 10018 or info@skyhorsepublishing.com.

Skyhorse® and Skyhorse Publishing® are registered trademarks of Skyhorse Publishing, Inc.®, a Delaware corporation.

Visit our website at www.skyhorsepublishing.com.

10 9 8 7 6 5 4 3 2 1

Library of Congress Cataloging-in-Publication Data is available on file.

ISBN: 978-1-62087-101-0

Printed in the United States of America

*To the Officers and Men of the
Second Division, United States Marines*

CONTENTS

To the Officers and Men of the
Second Division, United States Marines

CONTENTS

FOREWORD

This is the story of what one reporter saw and heard and thought during one battle. No official documents have been consulted. I have relied entirely upon my memory of what happened only a few days ago on Tarawa, and upon my notebooks, which I started filling assiduously as soon after the landing as I could dry them out.

Later it seemed ridiculous that I should have been scribbling in notebooks during that first day and a half on Tarawa when it seemed certain that I would never have the chance to write any stories from them. I suppose that it was because I felt quite helpless to do anything else. I had a feeling that I should have been doing something to help win the battle, if possible. Yet there was nothing prescribed in a war correspondent's list of duties. So I sat there on our twenty-foot beachhead, back against the slender seawall that was our protection, fulfilling the nearest thing I had to a duty, while men were being killed all around me. This volume is the result.

Any book about a battle is inadequate because it cannot impart to the reader a complete impression of what goes on in a battle. The same is true of photographs and films. There is not yet, for instance, any foolproof device for recording the sounds of battle, which are a thousand times more weird than anything the movies have conceived of. The whole island of Tarawa would tremble whenever our warships loosed a salvo of shells or a formation of our planes dropped their bombs upon it. If the bombs were close enough, the island seemed to jump from under us, and sand ran into our shoes. These things have to be felt to be fully realized. And, certainly, no one who has not been there can imagine the overwhelming, inhuman smell of five thousand dead who are piled and scattered in an area of less than one square mile.

This is an attempt to tell not only what happened on Tarawa, but also what men felt under the stress of the most violent battle that Americans had endured in this, the greatest war Americans have known.

ROBERT SHERROD

Washington
January, 1944

PRELUDE TO BATTLE

IN THE SUMMER OF 1943 the men who make the decisions about the strategy of the war decided to open a new theatre of war: the Central Pacific.

At that time we were already fighting the war against Japan in four theatres. In the South Pacific we were edging up from hard-won Guadalcanal into New Georgia and Rendova and Vella Lavella, and soon the bigger jump to Bougainville would be made. In the Southwest Pacific we laboriously pushed the Japanese out of one small settlement after another in the jungles of the north coast of New Guinea—the jump to New Britain was not to come for several months. The war in China was almost altogether an air war, whose supplies had to be flown over high, treacherous mountains. In the North Pacific U. S. soldiers had just killed the Japs on Attu and the Japs were about to make the riddance of the Aleutians complete by scurrying out of Kiska in the face of the proposed American and Canadian invasion.

When the decision to open the Central Pacific was made I was in the Aleutians. The Central Pacific sounded more exciting than anything I had seen in the war against Japan. In the first place, it would give us a chance to exercise the naval might which I could see building up all around me—for Kiska we had 135 ships, and that did not include the newer ones which were flowing out from the mainland shipyards in fairly steady streams. The Central Pacific, which is at least ninety-nine percent water, seemed an ideal place to use all this Navy.

Also, there was no malaria in the Central Pacific islands. Malaria had been a worse blight in the South Pacific jungles than Japanese bullets. And, while the average civilian would say that he vastly prefers malaria to bullets, many soldiers will swear they would rather take their chances on the bullets. Military-wise, a man knocked out by malaria is a casualty just as surely as one who has been wounded by shrapnel.

And there would be no snow or fog in the Central Pacific. I was sick of Aleutians weather. I was tired of flying in airplanes which took off in a little hole in the fog, hoping to find another hole in the fog at the end of the journey, tired of groping my way over tundra-covered mountains without being able to see more than thirty feet in any direction. In July I had boarded a cruiser for an eight-day task force patrol off Kiska. As I recall it, we saw our own protecting destroyers twice during the eight days. All that time they were within a few hundred yards on either side.

Thus, my enthusiasm for the opening of the Central Pacific, although I had no idea by what strategy we would eventually crush Japan. One might have looked at the various theatres in which we had begun fighting and assumed that Japan would be crushed, after long years, from all sides in a sort of medieval torture chamber.

I had to go to see my editors in New York before I undertook any more war-corresponding. But I was so interested in the Central Pacific that I went by way of Honolulu. At Adak I boarded a cruiser; seven days later, after watching the gray, dismal North Pacific change to the sparkling blue Central Pacific, I was in Pearl Harbor.

The naval strength I saw—though it was puny compared to what I saw later—convinced me that the Central Pacific was going to become the main news story in the Pacific war and, since nearly every reporter prefers to follow the main story, I wanted more than ever to see the curtain rise in the new theatre. I learned enough about the impending opening of the Central Pacific to convince my editors—without telling them what would happen—that here was a story worth covering.

The three September weeks and the 10,000-mile round trip between Honolulu and New York were a confusion of flying in an Army transport across the Pacific seated on mail bags—one would never imagine, just to look at it, that a mail bag can be so rocky—of battling priority officers, making four round-trip train trips (sometimes standing up) between office in New York and home in Washington, seeing editors and generals and admirals, kissing my children hello and goodbye, flying back from San Francisco to Honolulu on a Navy PB2Y which was rolling down the ramp into the water when I caught it. War correspondents' life expectancy may not be long, but what there is of it is rarely dull.

The big seaplane settled down on the waters of Pearl Harbor. I found a car and a telephone message waiting. I had three hours to board a carrier for "an important mission" with the Navy. My God, I said, are they going to invade the Jap-held islands so soon? Had the omission of battle on Kiska stepped up the timing so much more than I had expected?

But this was not the invasion of the Marshalls or the Gilberts —I did not know which we would hit first. It was a carrier-based raid on Wake Island, which could not fail to be a good story, because (1) it was the largest carrier task force ever assembled and (2) Wake Island was a place Americans would never forget.

The raid on Wake has not much to do with this story, which is about Tarawa. It was a gratifying experience to be able to say that we had sent a lot of planes and a lot of bombs against the Japs who held our island. It was especially gratifying to me to write, "I flew over in a dive bomber, in the second element of a wave of 180 planes." I had been in New Guinea early in the war when—in spite of the communiqués which daily told of our prowess—we often had only ten inadequate P-39's to send up against, or to flee from, the two daily raids of Jap bombers and Zeros. And it was gratifying to peer out of the gunner's seat of an SBD and watch it drop a bomb, in its dive from 14,500 to 700 feet, which fired a large oil tank and made the loveliest fire on the island. The Wake Island raid did not kill many Japs—you do not kill a man who is in a hole unless you drop a personal bomb on him—but it must have caused the Japs a great deal of trouble to rebuild what we destroyed there.

Back in Pearl Harbor after this satisfactory experience with a grand bunch of naval aviators, than whom there are no finer or more courageous people in the armed forces, I learned the assignments for the Gilbert Islands invasion. I was scheduled to go with the northern force of Army troops, the 165th New York Infantry, which would take Makin. This was disappointing because I knew by then that Tarawa not only would be a bigger show, but would involve Marines. I had never seen the Marines in action, whereas I had been with the Army several times. I mentioned this to Rear Admiral Richmond Kelly Turner, commander of the Amphibious Forces—a man with a rare understanding of the press and a keen perception of the political implications of war. Admiral Turner said he had no objection if my assignment were changed. Lieutenant Commander Ken McArdle, chief public relations officer for the Pacific Fleet in the absence of Commander Waldo Drake, was understanding about it, and he switched me to the southern, or Tarawa, force. Also switched were Keith Wheeler of the Chicago *Times,* an able newsman who had been on Attu, and Gilbert Bundy, a newly arrived young artist who was now working for King Features.

"You don't know how lucky you three are," said McArdle. I

was to chew over his words many times later, and to wonder what he meant. I never found out, exactly.

The assignment to Tarawa involved a long trip with a task force from one point in the Pacific to Base X where the naval forces—or part of them—would meet the Marines who were to do the invading. Wheeler, Bundy, and I were called one night at our lodgings at the original point and told to be packed and ready to depart at nine o'clock next morning.

Early next morning we drove out to the harbor. A public relations officer put us in one of the wood-paneled station wagons that always make the Navy seem like a country club, and drove us to the vessel that would transport us: one of the old battleships that had been repaired, rearmed, and virtually made over after its humiliation on December 7, 1941. I had seen this old battleship many times, but she might as well have been in another ocean for all I knew about the people inside her. I spoke to an officer of this remote nearness of ships at sea. He said, "About half this war one of my best friends has been on a nearby ship. A dozen times I could have thrown a rock and probably hit him. But I have never seen him."

The U. S. S. *Blisterbutt*, as the crew called her, and as I must call her too, was our home for the long days before we reached the rendezvous point in the South Pacific, was crowded, like most old ships which have been rearmed with many additional guns and gadgets. She carried more than two thousand officers and men—many hundreds more than she was built to carry. Her complement of officers was even more overcrowded than her complement of men, because old ships must train the officers who will run the new ships a-building. This crowding generally causes a ship's executive officer to scratch his head and ask himself "Where in the hell am I going to put them?" when faced with the necessity of providing quarters for war correspondents. Aboard the *Blisterbutt*, which was the flagship of the force, Rear Admiral Howard Kingman solved the problem when he moved up to his sea cabin and gave the correspondents his own quarters.

The *Blisterbutt* was on her way to battle. Her function was not the traditional function of the battleship: to sink the enemy fleet. Small hope of that. But she would shell Tarawa preparatory to the Marines' landing. Hundreds of her big shells, each weighing a ton or so, would blast the Jap fortifications, knock out the Jap seacoast guns, perhaps drive the Japs a little bit crazy.

The old *Blisterbutt* was slow, as all old battleships were slow in comparison to newer vessels like the *North Carolina* and *South Dakota*. This led to the fabrication of a cruel story which *Blisterbutt* men liked to tell on their ship. Just astern of us on the *Blisterbutt* pranced a majestic new battleship. It was as though a haughty race horse were forced to follow a plodding ox. From the *Blisterbutt* Admiral Kingman sent a blinker-light message to the captain of the new battleship, ordering him to stop that smoke from pouring out of his incinerator—the smoke might give away the task force to enemy patrol planes. The captain answered, so the story went, "Smoke unavoidable. Have been forced to cut out the boilers and burn garbage to slow down to your speed."

Life on the *Blisterbutt* was anything but exciting. Battleship men had begun to feel that they were as immune from enemy danger as a county clerk in Nebraska. Destroyers swarmed on every side like ants, protecting the force against submarines. There were airplane carriers to the portside and airplane carriers to the starboard, each carrier equipped with fast new fighters that could shoot down anything the Japs could put in the sky. If an enemy torpedo plane did manage to get through those fighters and through everybody else's anti-aircraft, then the old *Blisterbutt* had plenty of anti-aircraft guns of her own, and her gunners never hesitated to remind themselves that her gunnery records had always been among the best in the fleet.

If all these preventive measures failed, and a torpedo actually hit the ship—well, what was one torpedo to a mighty old fortress like *Blisterbutt?*

Therefore, our wartime voyage might as well have been a peacetime cruise in the South Seas. The brilliant sunlight, the far-reaching, incredibly blue Pacific, the soft breezes at evening and the Southern Cross in the sky—all these were no different than they had always been. For many there was not even much work to do. Since the *Blisterbutt* carried so many officers, and there was only so much work to be done without people getting in each other's way, some officers stood only one watch in six, i.e., worked only four hours a day. Most stood one watch in four.

But it was not like a peacetime cruise. "This is all very lovely," said a young junior-grade lieutenant, "but there are no women, and what is a cruise without women? And you can't go up to the bar and say, 'I think I'll have a dry Martini before dinner.' " And the executive officer, an able engineer and sailor, was hard. "I have to be," he said, "or some of these birds will relax." On the *Blisterbutt* we put on neckties before we went to dinner in the wardroom, though the thermometer hovered around 100. We didn't loll on the quarterdeck when we felt like it; sun-bathing was permissible only between noon and one o'clock. We never forgot about discipline, which in the U. S. Navy has long been synonymous with battleship.

The *Blisterbutt* hadn't had a fatal accident in fourteen years and she had had only four men killed by the two bomb hits she received at Pearl Harbor. But one day on the way to Tarawa, via Base X, her luck ran out. Two men were killed in unrelated accidents.

That she should have lost an officer and a man in one day's accidents was blamed by some superstitious sailors on the fact that a junior-grade lieutenant who had been on the ill-fated

carrier *Hornet* lost his lucky dollar on that day which happened
to be about one year after the sinking of the *Hornet.*

The ship's senior aviator, Lieutenant Harry P. Chapman, Jr.,
a quiet, popular Virginian, was the first casualty. He stepped
jauntily up the quarterdeck ladder, wearing his blue, long-billed
flyer's cap. His little patrol plane, an OS2U Kingfisher, was
already being warmed up, for launching off the catapult on a
routine patrol. The plane was trundled over to the catapult.
It was lifted onto the long catapult by a crane. Chapman climbed
into the cockpit and started revving up the engine.

But the plane's underside had been insecurely fastened to
the catapult slide. When the overhead cable was released, the
little OS2U started falling off the catapult toward the starboard side of the deck. I was standing only twenty feet in front
of Chapman. I could see the look of horror in his eyes when he
realized what was happening. He started to rise up out of his
seat. Then he realized it would do no good to try to jump. He
settled back, waiting for the crash.

Several sailors who were standing underneath tried bravely
to hold the plane in position by main strength. They jumped
out of the way just in time. Amid a rending of metal and glass
the plane crashed into the deck. The gunwales (side plates)
which rose eight inches above the deck's perimeter, cut into the
cockpit. The engine was knocked out of its frame. The plane
toppled into the water.

As we pulled away from the floating wreckage—battleships
do not stop in wartime—we could see one figure bob up. The
rear-seat radioman was safe, but there was no sign of Lieutenant
Chapman.

Within five minutes one of our destroyers was racing to the
wreckage, where it put a boat over. The destroyer stayed at the
scene forty minutes. A diver went under the plane, cutting his
arm severely on a piece of jagged aluminum. But nothing was
ever seen again of Chapman. The crash into the gunwales had

evidently knocked him unconscious and he undoubtedly was drowned.

The other accident was even more unusual. A young sailor named Kenneth Munson unaccountably had chosen to sleep under the loading platform of a main turret gun. When, in the darkness of early morning, the big gun was elevated, the platform crushed the seaman under the weight of its eighty tons. It was a wonder that any spark of life remained in him, but he lived and was conscious much of the fifteen hours remaining to him. I saw him in the sick bay an hour before he died, when medical corpsmen were feeding him oxygen to keep him alive. He cracked a joke, and there was a flicker of a sad smile on the faces of the three men about him.

Above all other things, Seaman Munson told the chaplain, he wanted to live. But he never had a chance. The doctor's report read: crushed pelvis, urethra ruptured, one lung punctured, belly wall punctured and intestines and liver forced up through the hole into the lung, skull fractured, brain probably full of hemorrhages. He was not in pain; the great physical shock of his mangling had mercifully put young Munson beyond pain.

Before he died the seaman, who had allowed himself to be listed on the ship's roll as a Protestant, revealed that he had been baptized and reared a Catholic. Through the Catholic chaplain, who told him that his time to die had come, the seaman made his peace with his God. He died at eight o'clock that night.

Quite a few days would elapse before the *Blisterbutt* reached port, so it was not feasible to hold the body for burial on land. Neither was there any reason for night burial—sometimes when casualties are heavy burial-at-sea ceremonies are held quietly and with brief prayers at night, lest the morale of the crew be disrupted by the sight of many shipmates going over the side for the last time. Preparations were made to bury the sailor at sea next morning at ten o'clock.

The body was clothed in the uniform of the day: blue dungarees. It was weighted by two five-inch shells (approximately one hundred pounds). It was sewed in canvas by the sailmaker, but the ancient custom of taking the last stitch through the nose of the deceased was omitted. Nor were coins placed in his mouth, as custom once dictated when sailors believed it was necessary to pay the boatman Charon for the body's passage across the river Styx.

The ceremony was brief, since we were sailing through submarine-infested waters, but it was impressive. Some time before ten o'clock on the day of the funeral two wooden carpenter's horses were placed on the starboard side of the quarterdeck. A detachment of armed Marines, distinguished from the sailors in blue by their khaki uniforms, stood at attention next to the horses. The ship's band stood aft of the Marines, their backs to the sea. Still further aft, about seventy-five officers faced forward. The most spectacular sight was the thousand or more dungaree-clad sailors who swarmed over the turret armor and out to the very ends of the big guns of the battleship, over the air-defense stations, the anti-aircraft turrets and guns, and the superstructure. It is doubtful if a dozen men on board had ever before seen a burial at sea. Everyone was there except those whose duty at that moment was to keep the ship running and the guns manned.

At 0940 the chaplain went below to the sick bay to bless the body, in the presence of the pallbearers, who were selected from the gunnery division of young Munson, who would never fire his big gun at Tarawa. The blessing was the 129th Psalm, which begins:

> *Out of the depths have I cried unto Thee, O Lord;*
> *Lord, hear my voice.*

and ends:

> *Eternal rest grant unto him, O Lord.*
> *And let perpetual light shine upon him.*

The pallbearers carried the body aft, the stocky young chaplain, Lieutenant Charles Covert, walking beside it, praying, "Come to his assistance, ye Saints of God! Meet him, ye Angels of the Lord. Receive his soul, and present it to the Most High. May Christ who called thee, receive thee; and may the Angels lead thee into the bosom of Abraham. Eternal rest grant unto him, O Lord!, and let perpetual light shine upon him."

When the pallbearers reached portside aft they had considerable difficulty lifting the body up the narrow ladder through the hatch, up to the quarterdeck. The band was softly playing *Nearer, My God, to Thee.* The body, covered by a large flag of the United States, was carried by the pallbearers across the quarterdeck and placed on the two wooden horses.

Now the service proper began. The hundreds of grave-faced men uncovered as Chaplain Covert, wearing a black cassock and white-lace surplice and black stole over his khaki officer's uniform, stood beside the body and prayed, almost inaudibly, for perhaps ten minutes, "Enter not into judgment with Thy servant, O Lord; for in Thy sight shall no man be justified, unless through Thee he find pardon for all his sins . . . Lord, have mercy on us. . . . Christ, have mercy on us. . . . Lord, have mercy on us."

The chaplain included in his prayers Lieutenant Chapman, an Episcopalian. Thus, instead of saying "deliver him," Father Covert prayed, "From the gates of Hell, deliver them, O Lord. May they rest in peace." And: "O God! To Whom it belongeth to show mercy and to spare, we humbly beseech Thee for the souls of Thy servants, whom Thou hast called out of this world, that Thou deliver them not into the hands of the enemy, not forget them forever; but command that they be received by Thy holy Angels. . . ."

Though the prayers in themselves followed the Catholic ritual almost as closely as if the funeral were being held on land, the chaplain interpolated some reference to the vast ocean whose bosom would receive the young sailor's body. "O God, through whose mercy the souls of the faithful find rest, be pleased to bless this watery grave. Send Thy Holy Angel to keep it; and loose from the bonds of sin the souls of all whose bodies lie beneath the waters of this sea, that they may ever rejoice in Thee with Thy saints. . . ."

At the end of the prayers the pallbearers lifted the flag, holding it a few inches above the canvas shroud which enveloped the sailor's body. The outboard carpenter's horse was removed and, tenderly, the pallbearers lowered the sailor's feet.

The Marine Guard, which had already about-faced toward the sea, snapped smartly to "Present Arms!" More than a thousand officers and men brought their right hands to their foreheads in a farewell salute as the American sailor moved off the stretcher from underneath the flag and silently disappeared into the sparkling waters of the blue Pacific. Father Covert made the sign of the Cross, and said, "May the blessing of Almighty God, the Father, Son, and Holy Ghost descend upon you and remain forever. Amen." The Marines brought their rifles to "Order Arms!"

The Marine captain barked, "Ready! Aim! Fire!" The first volley from the Marines' Garand rifles cracked over the waters. Then a second and a third. The bugler sweetly sounded *Taps*, which is as stirring a piece of music as ever was written.

The band played *Onward, Christian Soldiers*. The officers and men stepped from the deck into the bowels of the ship, back to the business of war. That afternoon the padre said a mass for young Munson. The following Sunday there was a memorial service for Lieutenant Chapman.

Aboard the *Blisterbutt* there were, as passengers, four "foreigners"—what a strange word for such men!—who were to play an important part in the Tarawa invasion. All were British subjects, shipmasters who had for many years sailed the waters around the Gilbert Islands. Now their duty would be to navigate those waters for the invasion, to board the leading ships and take our force into the virtually uncharted waters. Having only halfway dependable, hundred-year-old guidebooks, we had to place the largest force the Pacific had seen in the hands of mariners who relied upon their memories. Fortunately, those mariners and memories were good.

Two of the "foreigners," Lieutenants Page and Webster, were transferred—via breeches buoy—to destroyers early in the voyage, and I never got to know them well. But I listened long and fascinated to grizzled, old Karl Tschaun and bright-eyed, ruddy James Forbes.

Karl Tschaun was born in Latvia, then a part of Russia. At nineteen he went to England and two years later, at twenty-one, to Australia. From 1910 until the mid-1930's he had one job: a sailor in the service of the great South Seas trading firm, Burns Philp & Co. His last command had been a twin-engined, three-masted barkentine.

James Forbes was a Scotsman who became a New Zealander. For several years before the war he had commanded the British Government vessel, the *Nimanoa*, which cruised regularly among the Gilbert Islands, bringing government supplies and mail, carrying officials from one island to another.

Of the Gilbert Islands I knew only that they lay across the equator, extending some four hundred miles from southeast to northwest, and that we were about to attack Tarawa and Makin, where the Japs had their only sizable concentrations. Messrs. Tschaun and Forbes set out to teach me something about the Gilberts:

There are sixteen islands in the Gilbert group, from Arorae in the southeast to Little Makin—not to be confused with its more important neighbor, Makin or Butaritari—in the north-west. The British colonial administration for the Gilbert and Ellice Islands was, before the Japanese invasion early in 1942, on Ocean Island, which is not a part of either group but sits off to the west by itself. Most important of the Gilbert Islands was Tarawa—accented on the first syllable, *Tar*—which was the islands' port of entry and the residence of the senior administrative officer and the senior medical officer. About one-fourth of the Gilberts' one hundred whites and forty Asiatics had lived on Tarawa, about 3,000 of the 27,000 Micronesian natives.

The Tarawa atoll is made up of twenty-five small islands and the coral reef passageway between them is dry at low tide, so that it is possible to walk from one to another. These twenty-five islands form a reversed L, eighteen miles north to south and twelve miles across the base east to west. An underwater coral reef, characteristic of all atolls, completes the triangle and encloses a large lagoon which is navigable by vessels of any size.

Most important of the twenty-five islands of Tarawa was Betio—called Bititu on some maps—at the southwest corner of the atoll. There the British officials maintained their headquarters. Burns Philp & Co. had a warehouse there and maintained a commercial radio station. On the maps Betio has the shape of a bird lying on its back, tail tapering off to the east. This appearance is heightened by the pier which juts out like a leg five hundred yards from the bird's belly. Betio is only two and one-quarter miles long, and at its widest point is only half a mile wide. The total area of the island is something less than one square mile. Betio was our target. Plainly, we were unlikely to find much of our target undefended.

I asked Karl Tschaun about the natives.

"They are fine people," he said, "very intelligent, husky—you wouldn't think coconuts and fish would produce such healthy specimens—and very kindly. They are—or were—a happy people, who sang a lot. Had very good voices. They are brown-skinned people, Micronesians. Not as light as Polynesians, not as dark as Melanesians.

"You know," the old ship's captain continued, "these people got along very well. They liked the British rule. Each village had its own *kaubure* [pronounced cow-berry] or council. And a native magistrate administered justice, except in capital crimes, where the British courts took over. The natives had only one crop, copra from the coconuts, and I guess they produced maybe four thousand tons a year. It brought only four or five pounds for the ton, so it's obvious that nobody was getting rich off the Gilberts.

"I'm afraid we are going to kill a lot of the natives when we bomb and shell the place. Maybe we already have killed some in the bombing raids. I'm just hoping the Japs moved the natives off the islands where they had military installations. And I'm afraid of what the Japs might have done to the natives. Take the Marshall Islands—what a crying shame it was to hand those people over to the Japs after the last war! The Marshall natives —and I knew them well until the Japs took over the islands and shut the rest of the world off from them—were like pups that used to be happy until they were beaten into frightened, trembling dogs. The Japs made them bow down every time they met a Jap.

"The Marshallese could not stand humiliation. When the Japs flogged a native he died of shame. The doctors actually could not determine the cause of death—there was no apparent physical reason for it. And every time a native died off the Japs imported a Jap to take his place. I understand the population of the Marshalls has decreased steadily since the Japs moved in on them. The Marshalls have always been so many poor, small islands compared to the Gilberts, anyway."

Said Captain Forbes, "The Gilbertese were proud too. Their dignity always had to be respected. The worst thing you could do to a Gilbertese was to ridicule him before other natives. You could clout him if he was wrong about something, and he'd laugh. But to treat him unjustly insulted his dignity and he was never the same again.

"I'll tell you something else about the Gilbertese that might give you an idea," said Forbes. "They placed a high price on virtue. The penalty for adultery used to be death. The two principals were placed in a canoe without oars, food, or water, and set adrift on the eastward side of the island, with no hope of ever reaching land. The British discouraged such severity after they came.

"The world doesn't know much about these Gilbert Islands, but there is a lot of romance connected with their history. I used to like these islands very much—I got to know the South Seas from Auckland to Butaritari like the back of my hand, and there is none of it more fascinating than the Gilberts. Nothing but little spits of coral and sand studded with coconut palms. You can throw a rock across most of the islands. But the weather is fine—not too hot, in spite of being on the equator. Nearly always a cool breeze.

"There was an old man named Isaac Handley who lived on Tarawa. In fact, I hope he is still alive. He was seventy-eight years old and he refused to leave when the others left. He was a Liverpool boy who went to sea at the age of twelve, became well-to-do, and finally built himself a fine home in Sydney. But he preferred the Gilberts to his fine home in Sydney. When the Japs came and the others left, he just said he thought he would stay—he had been there so long.

"You may be interested in how the whites who got out of the Gilberts got away," the little Scotsman went on. "The Japs landed at three o'clock one morning on Tarawa. They were very nervous and appeared anxious to leave as soon as possible. They looted the stores, but left some food for the eight or ten whites remaining, including the Burns Philp manager, the medical officer, and shipmaster Edward Harness, who had succeeded me as master of the *Nimanoa*. Then the Japs turned the natives into the stores and left about eight o'clock. Before they left they took Harness aboard the *Nimanoa* and cautioned him against any monkey business, but allowed him to pack his bag.

"He managed to smuggle his sextant and log tables among his clothes, when the Japs weren't looking. He ran the *Nimanoa* on a reef and the Japs blew her up. Two oil tanks exploded but her hull and some ribs were left intact. All the Japs wanted to do was make certain that the whites didn't get away.

"But Harness and the others managed to find an engine and hide it from the Japs. And to cover a twenty-foot boat with palm leaves. Three days after the first Japs had left a Jap Navy party came ashore. The first Japs had been tough and insolent —they had killed two natives who had been loosed from the insane asylum; one of them had been bayoneted in the medical officer's house and had dragged himself over the dining-room floor, bleeding profusely from the stomach—but this naval party was very polite. The Jap lieutenant even told Harness he was sorry he lost his boat.

"Then the Navy inspection party left Tarawa, too. Harness and the others, excepting old man Handley and Jim Smith, who also elected to stay, saw their last chance to get away. They set out in the small boat they had hidden under the palm fronds, installed the engine they had put away and set out for Suva, thirteen hundred miles to the south. But first they stopped at Nonouti—it's pronounced No-nooch—which is the fifth Gilbert island to the south of Tarawa. There they found six American sailors who had been on the *Donerail*, which was sunk off Pearl Harbor during the first few days of the war. They took on the sailors, who were in pretty bad shape, and kept going until they reached Suva. When the Japs came back again there were still some whites in the Gilberts—a few New Zealand soldiers who manned lookout posts, and the priests of the Catholic missions—I think all the London Missionary Society people got out all right.

"By the way, those old Catholic missionaries were remarkable people. Mostly French. I used to see a lot of them in the Gilberts. When they came out to the Gilberts they expected to stay there until they died. They lived the same life the natives did, ate the same food, and devoted their lives to the natives. I remember one of them particularly. He had had leprosy and had spent seven years at the colony in the Fijis getting cured. Once

I had to collect lepers from the Gilberts and take them to the colony. It was a horrible job. Some of the lepers were old people. But some were children who had to be taken from their parents by force. I put these lepers in a sort of cage that I had built on the stern of my ship. I fixed it up the best I could. Then I tried to get somebody to take care of the lepers during the trip to Suva. I had a hard time.

"This old priest—he lived on Kuria—said he would go. During the trip to Suva he passed the food to the lepers in the cage. He read to them in their native tongue and did everything he could to help them. He even slept on the deck next to the cage. Later I saw him often on Kuria—that's another one of the Gilbert Islands. We always had a drink together.

"Another old priest had a flowing white mane. Another was called 'Mossy Teeth'—he never bathed or shaved and he certainly never used a toothbrush. You couldn't stand within ten feet of him, he was so dirty. But the natives loved him."

We got to talking about the history of the Gilbert Islands, which were soon to be injected violently into American history. According to Captain Tschaun's copy of the pre-war New Zealand publication, *Sailing Directions on Navigation Between the Islands and Atolls of the Gilbert Group,* the first of the sixteen islands to be discovered was Nikunau, one of the southernmost of the islands. A British Commander Byron came across it in the *Dolphin* in 1765. But Captains Gilbert and Marshall were the principal pioneers; each named a group of islands after the other. In 1788 Gilbert in the *Charlotte* and Marshall in the *Scarborough* discovered Abemama, Kuria, Aranuka, Tarawa, Abaiang, Butaritari, and Makin. A Captain Bishop of the brig *Nautilus* discovered Nonouti and Tabiteuea in 1799. Captain Patterson in the *Elizabeth* sighted Arorae and Miana in 1809, and Captain Duperry of the corvette *Coquille* discovered Marakei in 1824.

"You probably don't know it," said James Forbes, "but you Americans had a hand in developing the Gilberts. In 1841 two ships belonging to the United States Exploring Expedition, the *Peacock* and the *Flying Fish*, commanded by Commander Wilkes and Captain Hudson, were out here in the Gilberts. They mapped and charted reefs and anchorages around many of the islands.

"And," he added, "those are the charts that are still used.

"There have been other Americans in the Gilberts from time to time. The census of 1931 showed one American Negro among the 26,000 natives of the Gilberts. I never found out what happened to him. Then, back in the nineteenth century, there were a couple of sailors who deserted their ships—the Gilberts were always a great place for beachcombers. One of them was an Irishman and the other was an American. When a British ship came by, as one did once in a while, both of them claimed to be Yanks. If an American ship sailed through, they were both British subjects, therefore immune to any regulations. They lived like kings and ruled their island—it was Marakei—with iron hands."

The old *Blisterbutt* splashed through the deadening heat of the South Pacific with great monotony. A battleship cruise can be very dull when there is no prospect of action. Sometimes the convoy would head east; another day we would find ourselves mysteriously going west or north. We must have crossed the international dateline three times; finally we lost count of whether it was Thursday or Friday, and nobody cared very much. One day I asked Forbes how the British happened to take over the Gilbert Islands.

"That's an interesting story, as I heard it from the old-timers," he said. "There was an old tyrant of a king on Abemama—that's the loveliest of the islands, I think. His name was Timbinoka, and he cut men to pieces if they sneezed in his presence. Timbinoka * began reaching out, so Captain Davis of

* The spelling, like all spelling of native Gilbertese names, is a compromise. It might be Timtinaka, because p, t, and b are usually slurred into nothingness. Abemama is often spelled Apemama—the b or p is little more than a pause between the two vowels.

H. M. S. *Royalist* sailed in and proclaimed a British protectorate over the group in 1892.

"Robert Louis Stevenson had a run-in with Timbinoka. Stevenson came to the Gilberts in search of a climate to rest his tubercular lungs. He landed a horse, too, which scared hell out of the natives on Abemama—they had never seen one. Timbinoka was too much for Stevenson, so he packed up and sailed away for Samoa.

"Later, when Stevenson wrote *The South Seas* he referred to George Murdoch as 'a niggardly recluse,' favorite of the native king. Well, George was a sort of handyman for Timbinoka at that time—he had come out from Scotland when he was nine or ten. But he later became District Officer, and he never forgave Stevenson."

"You Yanks think the South Seas are not romantic," said James Forbes. "Well, that's because you're naturally the homesickest people on earth and because you haven't seen much of the South Seas except the jungles and mud and rain and malaria. War is always fought in the worst possible places; the Central Pacific will be a little better, so far as the weather is concerned.

"In peacetime the South Seas are a wonderful place, though. I remember a friend of mine, mate on a trading schooner that was in Suva. Well, Suva is the capital of the South Seas. It used to have everything, including all the vices, even an All-Nations Street.

"This mate liked to dance, he did. He went to a dance one night at the Grand Pacific Hotel—that's the place everybody heads for in Suva. Ever been there?"

I said I had been in the G. P. H., as everybody calls it, in August, 1942. It was full of American soldiers and sailors drinking whisky, served by dour, barefoot Indian waiters, and at the bar stood lusty New Zealand soldiers, drinking beer; and there were three newly arrived, homesick American Army nurses sitting on the cool porch talking to a press association correspondent, refusing to drink anything.

"Well, that shows what war will do to a place," said Captain Forbes. "The G. P. H. used to be a real showplace. All the American tourists who came in on the Matson Liners went to the dances at the G. P. H. There was a boatload there the evening my friend went to dance. He met this attractive American woman—not elderly, but mature, I'd say between thirty-five and forty. They had a few drinks. Between dances they took a spin out to Suva Point. Then they danced some more. He told her he was mate on a trading schooner. She was sim-ply thril-led; wouldn't he show her the schooner? So he took her out to the schooner.

"The lady sailed away next day, but she started to write letters to my friend. She wanted to chuck it all and come out to live with him. He used to answer her letters and play along with her, just for fun. Then one day he got a letter that scared the lights out of him, from a lawyer in the States, saying this correspondence must cease. The lady's husband had found out about it and was quite angry. The correspondence ceased, forthwith. A long time afterward my friend saw the lady's picture in a big society magazine he happened to pick up. He didn't know she was so important. But, I tell you, this South Sea does something to people."

That was a fine voyage on the old *Blisterbutt*. But, when action is in the offing, even the best of voyages, with the best of companions, begins to pall. The worst part about any war is the waiting, and even the most patient of Marines—who are likely to see more action than anybody else—begin to fret after days, weeks, and months of preparing, watching, and waiting for a few hours or a few days of combat. Americans hate to wait. The Japs said the chief characteristics of American soldiers were optimism and impatience, and, whereas a Jap sniper stoically would wait all day for one particular shot at one particular officer before he gave away his position and got himself killed, the American would say, "The hell with this waiting," then break out his tommy gun to kill all the Japs he could before trying to make a break.

Thus, we were glad to reach the end of our journey. In the last few days we correspondents had written whatever stories occurred to us during the voyage, we had read a book a day, we had talked to all the officers and many of the crew. We had drunk three or four Coca-Colas at a sitting, just for the excitement of rolling dice with the chaplain to see who would pay for them—the padre invariably lost. In the last few days we found ourselves, at about five in the afternoon, speculating on what three-year-old Grade B movie would be shown—for the second time during the voyage—in the wardroom after dinner.

Late one afternoon in November we reached the spot where we would rendezvous with the Second Marine Division, which was coming up from New Zealand. The rendezvous point was Base X in the South Pacific. I had spent most of the past two years in the Pacific and I knew what a big ocean it was, but it occurred to me that a battle on the equator had taken me from New York to San Francisco to Honolulu to a jungle base in the South Pacific. Already I had traveled thousands of miles for the Battle of Tarawa, not counting five thousand more on the Wake Island side trip, and the battleground was still some hundreds of miles away.

THE MARINES

LIKE OTHER BASES built early in the war, X had settled down. Hastily cleared out of the jungle when the Japs seemed to be on the verge of cutting southward from Guadalcanal to New Caledonia, thus periling the thin supply line to Australia, X was now on the way to becoming a rear area. Life was crude—nothing like the "country clubs" at Honolulu, Noumea, Kodiak, and such places that had apparently been forever by-passed by the war—but it was not unpleasant.

Now that the base had been built to sizable proportions, the airfields built, the anti-aircraft guns unlimbered, there was not so much of the backbreaking labor that must go into a new base. The soldiers and sailors had enough beer most of the time; once in a while they saw a good movie at one of the open-air theatres; they lived in quarters that were comfortable enough, many of them in Pacific huts or Quonset huts modified for hot weather.

Certainly, they wanted to go home, or anywhere. Who wants to sit out the war in a clearing in the jungle, a million miles from nowhere? Many of them counted the days. When the war correspondents finally got ashore and went into Ensign Parsons' office, they asked politely how long he had been on Base X.

"I've been here only seven months," said Mr. Parsons, "but some of the men have been here about eighteen months."

"Eighteen months, hell," said a dungaree-clad quartermaster. "It will be nineteen months day after tomorrow."

We had to wait several days for the arrival of the Marines in the transports. The Officers Club was as pleasant a place as might be found on the edge of a jungle in the South Pacific, and the bar was open two hours each afternoon, serving the best rum collinses south of the equator. The ice-making machine at the bar was a source of wonderment to the newly arrived officers. It spewed forth in unending succession thin slivers which, when placed in a glass, gave forth such an appearance as to cause one officer to ask, "What am I drinking, bourbon and noodles?" But it was cold.

During the wait at Base X we met the men who would run the Tarawa show: Rear Admiral Harry Hill, the lean, handsome commander of the Southern (Tarawa) Amphibious Force; Major General Julian C. Smith, sensitive, kindly Marylander who commanded the Second Marine Division; and Colonel Merritt A. Edson, chief of staff of the division.

Of these Edson was best-known. With his famed First Raider Battalion, he was generally credited with saving Guadalcanal during the fierce fighting of September 13 and 14, 1942—an action which won him the Congressional Medal of Honor and the British Distinguished Service Order. No man in the Marine Corps was more highly regarded by the professionals than Edson. A husky, intense blond, he was slightly hunch-shouldered, and his soft voice did not belie his steel-blue killer's eyes. He hated the Japs, as only men who have met them in combat hate them. Whenever, during his hour-long lecture to the correspondents the day before we left Base X, he used the phrases, "killing Japs," or "knocking off Nips," his eyes seemed to light up, and he smiled faintly.

"We cannot count on heavy naval and air bombardment to kill all the Japs on Tarawa, or even a large proportion of them," said Colonel Edson, to the more-than-mild surprise of some of us who had been listening to the claims of some battleship gunnery officers—one claimed there would not even be a land mass for the Marines to land on after the big guns had finished with Tarawa.

"Neither can we count on taking Tarawa, small as it is, in a few hours. You must remember the inevitable slowness of ground action," added Edson. The colonel talked for an hour. He went into the details of the Tarawa operation, pointing out which battalions would land where. He gave us the timing schedules of the naval guns and planes which would shower Tarawa in less than four hours with the most concentrated mass of high explosives in all history—the ships would fire 2,000 tons of shells, ranging from 16-inch battleship shells weighing more than a ton apiece to 5-inch destroyer bullets weighing a little over fifty pounds; the planes would drop 1,500 tons of bombs (actually, this figure was cut down somewhat—we were told after the battle that, not counting the four days' previous bombardment, 900 tons of bombs actually fell on Tarawa in the pre-landing action). The correspondents finally had been notified officially about Tarawa.

"Some of the battalion commanders think we can take it in three hours," smiled Edson, "but I think it may take a little longer. These Nips are surprising people."

I asked General Smith about his division. He was very proud of it. "I think they will do well. They are a fine bunch of fighting men. And guess how many are absent without leave? Just sixteen out of seventeen thousand, and only four of them were last-day cases which failed to show up when we left New Zealand. You'll have to look a long way to find a better record than that; you can usually figure on one percent missing the boat when it is about to sail into combat.

"There's one thing about an operation of this kind that most people don't realize," Julian Smith continued, "and that is the vast amount of preparation involved. There are a million things that must be attended to before the division commander can say, 'Ready.' We started planning this Tarawa operation last August—we were told on August first that the Central Pacific had been chosen as the next theatre, and we were well into the plans two weeks later.

"Look at the special training the men had to get—beachhead landings, night fighting, various kinds of new equipment. Then the equipment had to come from many thousands of miles. Some of the ships we are going to use weren't even built when we started preparing. Some of the LST's [landing ships for tanks] we will use won't meet us until we get outside Tarawa. I'm afraid the people back home do not know what careful planning and precise timing are required to fight even one battle in a war."

Before we left Admiral Hill's battleship Merritt Edson spoke up, "One more thing I forgot to tell you. The troops on Tarawa are a special navy landing force—what the newspapers call Jap Marines or Imperial Japanese Marines. That means they are the best Tojo's got."

The correspondents drew their assignments. Four of us were assigned to the transport which would carry the Second Battalion of the Second Regiment of the Second Division: myself; red-headed William Hipple of the Associated Press, a former Honolulu newspaperman; Bundy the artist; and Don Senick, Fox newsreelman who had long since acquired the nickname, "Fearless Fosdick."

Our battalion was scheduled to hit the center of the landing area, with another assault battalion on either side of us. "I see that we get shot at from both sides," observed Hipple, cheerfully. As a matter of fact, all three battalions were to be shot at from both sides, though ours was to take the heaviest casualties of all the battalions that finally landed on Tarawa—about sixty percent.

But that was still days away. Before sailing out of the South

Pacific there was one more full-scale dress rehearsal. A small boat took us out to the Navy transport, which I shall call the *Blue Fox*. The *Blue Fox* was stacked to the gunwales with Marines. They filled the holds, they poured over onto the decks. They were restless, after more than two weeks already aboard, but never during the voyage to Tarawa did I hear one complaint.

Hipple and I were assigned to a small bunkroom which already contained five junior officers, first and second lieutenants and a Marine Gunner (warrant officer). It was not only hot; it was steaming. How we slept in that torrid bunkroom I do not know, but we actually managed to sleep about fourteen hours out of each twenty-four. In the daytime there were two portholes that could be opened, but at night these had to be closed, and there was a blackout screen with an airscoop attached for only one of these portholes. That let in a little air, but even the ocean night air in the South Pacific seemed like so much steam. We lay in bed and sweated without pause all night long. Then, in the daytime, we swallowed many salt tablets to restore the salt we had lost through perspiration during the night.

I matched with Hipple to see which of us would hit the beach in the battalion commander's landing boat, which of us in the battalion executive officer's boat. He drew the c.o.'s boat, which was to go in shortly after the first wave. My boat would reach shore with the fifth wave, some minutes after the first wave.

On the morning of the rehearsal, which would be held on an island before we proceeded to Tarawa, we were awakened at 0230. Breakfast in the broiling officer's wardroom was pancakey eggs and coffee. Some time before dawn the boats of the first wave were hoisted over the side, filled with the Marines who were to have the toughest job in the military book: landing on an enemy beach in the face of hostile fire.

The boat which I was to ride into the beach for this rehearsal—and, later, into Tarawa—drew alongside shortly after five o'clock. We climbed over the side of the transport and scampered down the rope cargo net, being careful to grasp the vertical ropes of the net—lest the man just above step on your fingers. There were about thirty-two of us in the Higgins boat, mostly staff personnel of the battalion. Senior officer in the boat was Major Howard Rice of Detroit, a short, pleasant Regular Marine who worried about his falling hair. One of the favorites of the battalion who was in our boat was young Dr. M. M. Green of Reno, a Navy doctor whose escapades in New Zealand had fastened on him the nickname: "Greeno the Mareeno."

Some were medical corpsmen ("pelicans"), but most of the enlisted men in the boat were communications personnel: operators of portable radios, wiremen, and runners—many an old Marine still puts absolute faith in these fearless message carriers who operate between the front lines when radios go haywire and the enemy cuts the telephone lines. For this rehearsal they were a rollicking crew until most of them fell asleep during the two hours of circling and circling, waiting for the waves of boats to form. One poor fellow was seasick over the side of the boat. His pals showed him no mercy.

"How would you like a nice piece of fat pork?" one of them chirped, and the seasick Marine lost the rest of his breakfast. "Take a drink of warm salt water," advised another.

The Marines also liked to talk about their life in New Zealand. One Marine came in for a lot of ribbing because from the final maneuver on a desolate New Zealand beach he had returned to the transport and asked the corpsmen for a venereal prophylactic, much to the envy of his fellows who asked him what on earth he had been doing. Seems that his outpost far up "front" had been crossed by some friendly Maori girls.

The Marines apparently had been heroes to the New Zealanders, especially to the New Zealand girls. Several hundred Second Division men—some said two hundred, some said a thousand—had married New Zealand girls. And there had been plenty of women to go around, a rare state of affairs in this womanless war. "Hey, Jones," shouted one Marine who stood

near the stern of the boat, "tell 'em about that old dame about
thirty-six or thirty-seven you had out in Wellington that sneezed
and her teeth fell in her beer."

Major Rice ordered everybody to duck low in the boat for
the last couple of hundred yards. The boat driver put on full
steam and after a few minutes we heard the boat crunch on the
sand; the ramp in the bow was lowered and we dashed the remaining twenty-five yards through knee-deep water. We had
made our last practice landing. The troops deployed into the
jungle, some as deep as eight hundred yards—the maximum
width of Tarawa. Overhead some planes, but not nearly as many
as we would actually have on Tarawa, made practice dives and
strafing runs. Behind us came other waves of men who rushed
ashore when the white wakes of their boats had melted into the
land.

Ashore I met the man who commanded the combat team, the
three assault battalions. His headquarters had been set up just
as they would be set up on Tarawa, in the same relative spot,
using the same telephones and radio and staff who would per-
form the same functions under enemy fire. Colonel David Shoup
—he had been promoted from lieutenant colonel that day—had
assumed command only yesterday, relieving an ailing regimental commander almost on the eve of battle.

He was an interesting character, this Colonel Shoup. A squat,
red-faced man with a bull neck, a hard-boiled, profane shouter
of orders, he would carry the biggest burden on Tarawa. On
his judgment and his ability would depend the lives of several
thousand men and, ultimately perhaps, whether or not we won
the battle.

David M. Shoup had been born on a farm near Battleground,
Indiana, thirty-nine years ago. He had won a scholarship at
De Pauw University, where he was an A student. I learned all
this later. As a matter of fact, Colonel Shoup's grammar, which
had not the slightest thing to do with his winning or losing the
battle, was more like that of a Marine sergeant who had never

passed the eighth grade. He had joined the Marines as a second lieutenant soon after he finished college in 1926. He had served in the usual Navy yards and aboard the battleship *Maryland*, and in Shanghai, Pekin, and Tientsin. Early in the war he had commanded a battalion in Iceland, and lately he had been Operations Officer of the Second Division. He was the tough Marine officer in the best tradition, and he had the greatest faith in the Marines' ability to succeed in anything they undertook.

❡ Finally the transport was on its way to Tarawa, surrounded by many other transports and by scores of warships: battleships, aircraft carriers, heavy cruisers, light cruisers, countless destroyers, mine sweepers, and the various auxiliary craft necessary for landing operations. Whether this naval might induced a general feeling of security, or whether the fifty-five percent of the Marines who were already veterans bred confidence in the others, I do not know. Maybe the heat simply made them lethargic. But there was no more excitement aboard the *Blue Fox* than if so many men were on their way to the factory on a Tuesday morning.

Several men told me that they had a lot of confidence in the Navy. These men were part of a regiment that had been on Tulagi and Guadalcanal from the start, and their confidence had been shaken when the Navy pulled out after it had lost four cruisers, leaving the Marines without much food and without much visible hope of staying alive. The military necessity of pulling the Navy out of Guadalcanal did not even occur to the average Marine, whose philosophy is based on the simple premise that "when the other fellow is in trouble you don't go off and leave him." "But now," said Pfc. Herman Lewis, who quit his Johnstown newspaper job to enlist in the Marines, "we look at all this Navy, and it gives us confidence. When we looked out at the stretch of water between Tulagi and Guadalcanal and didn't see *anything*, we didn't feel so good." This renewed confidence in the Navy was shared by enlisted men and officers alike. One of the higher ranking officers on board told me, "The Navy is really going to take some chances this time, even if they lose some ships."

I spent a lot of time studying the Marines. They looked like any group of ordinary, healthy young Americans. The range of their background was as broad as America: farmers, truck drivers, college students, runaway kids, rich men's sons, orphans, lawyers, ex-soldiers. One day Lieutenant William B. Sommerville, the battalion supply officer, himself a Baltimore lawyer, was showing me around the ship. On deck we passed a Marine corporal with a bandaged thumb. Sommerville stopped and asked what happened.

"I let my air hose get away from me," grinned the corporal. We walked on. "That guy," said Sommerville, "was a county judge in Texas when he enlisted."

All these Marines were volunteers. Only now, several months after voluntary enlistments had been stopped—to the unconcealed disgust of old-line Marine sergeants who had from time immemorial been able to fall back on the final, scathing word, "Nobody asked you to be a Marine, bub"—were the first Marine draftees being sent overseas as replacements.

The Marines ate the same emergency rations that soldiers ate in battle. They used the same weapons. They came from the same places.* They went to the same schools. What, then, had gained the Marines a reputation as fighting men far excelling any attributed to the average young U. S. citizen in a soldier's uniform?

I had been curious about this question for at least a year before the United States went to war. I recalled a White House press

* With some differences. A glance at the roster of men aboard the *Blue Fox* showed a preponderance of Midwesterners, Southerners, and Californians, and almost no New Englanders. Thus, of 1,618 Marines and attached naval units aboard, 115, or seven percent, were from Texas, whereas Texas holds just under five percent of the U. S. population. But I had seen no units overseas in this war, outside some National Guard outfits, to which Texas had not contributed more than her pro-rata share. Texans were sometimes immodest on this point, but their boast was well-founded.

conference in June, 1940, when President Roosevelt said angrily that a year of military training would be good for the molly-coddled youth of the United States—at least, it would teach them to live with their fellow men. The weeks I spent on maneuvers with the Army in the swamps of Louisiana and in the Carolina hills did not serve to ease my fears that perhaps we had grown too soft to fight a war; at that time some low-moraled outfits were threatening to desert, rather than stay in the Army. Almost none of them deserted, but the threat was an unhealthy sign, and it could not be blamed entirely on poor leadership.

When I came back to the United States after half a year in Australia, in August, 1942, I went around Cassandra-fashion, crying, "We are losing the war—you don't realize it, but we are losing the war!" I talked to several men at the top of the Army and Navy. I went to the White House and sang my mournful tune to the President. To bear bad tidings is a very rocky road to popularity, but I felt that somebody had to do it.

What worried me was not our productive ability, although it was barely in evidence at the time. I knew we could make the machines of war. But I didn't know whether we had the heart to fight a war. Our men who had to do the fighting didn't want to fight. Their generation had been told in the all-important first ten years, in its teens, and at the voting age that it was not necessary to fight. Sometimes it almost seemed that they had been taught that peace was more important than honor. Our men just wanted to go home.

I could not forget my conversation one chilly August day in a room in Lennon's Hotel in Brisbane. My companion was an Army general, a friend of many years. I asked his opinion of the American soldier. He became very depressed. He said, "I'm afraid, Bob. I'm afraid the Americans of this generation are not the same kind of Americans who fought the last war."

In the spring of 1943 I went to the Aleutians. The Battle of Attu in its early stages was not well handled. Our equipment was poor. Nearly fifteen hundred men became casualties from exposure because of their poor equipment, and because their leaders allowed them to be pinned down for days in icy water on the floor of Massacre Valley. But the Battle of Attu did not make me feel any worse. In this primitive, man-against-man fighting enough of our men rose up to win. I thought I learned a lesson on Attu which probably applied to all armies: not all soldiers are heroes—far from it; the army that wins, other things being fairly equal, is the army which has enough men to rise above duty, thus inspiring others to do their duty. There were many such Americans on Attu—men received the fairly commonplace Silver Star for deeds that would have earned a Congressional Medal of Honor earlier in the war. I thought I learned another lesson on Attu: no man who dies in battle dies in vain. There is no time for mourning during a battle, but the after-effect a soldier's battlefield grave has on his comrades is sometimes overpowering. Five weeks after the Battle of Attu ended, a memorial service was held for the six hundred Americans who died there. No man of the 17th, 32nd, or 4th Regiments who attended this service is likely ever to forget that hundreds of men scaled Attu's summer-clad brown peaks to pick wild mountain flowers, with which they made wreaths for the graves of their brothers-in-arms. Could the living fail to gain from their own dead an inspiration which would sustain them in future battles? Can one American watch another die in his cause, by his side, without realizing that that cause must be worth while, and, therefore, must be pursued to a victorious end, whatever the cost?

This was the hard way of gaining an education, but, since we in America had made such an abominable job of educating a generation, we had no other method during the first two years of war. Therefore, our soldiers showed up poorly in their first battles. The number of "war neuroses" or "shell-shock" cases among them simply reflected the fact, in my opinion, that they were not mentally prepared to bridge the vast gap between the comforts of peace and the horrors of war. In other words, they had been brought up to believe that it was only necessary to wish for peace to have peace, and the best way to avoid war was to turn our heads the other way when war was mentioned. I had no words to describe the effect the first bombs and bullets had on many of the men educated in such fashion. Fortunately, most of them recovered their equilibrium after the initial shock. Fortunately, there were signs after two years of war that the oncoming generation of soldiers—those who had been conscious for two years of the nearness of war to them—would go into battle better prepared, better educated.

I thought Attu could be told in the story of the sergeant. On top of one of those snowy, marrow-chilling peaks in May, 1943, the platoon leader, a second lieutenant, ordered the sergeant to take a squad and go over there and knock out that Jap machine-gun nest. The sergeant just stared. His mouth was open. He was horrified. He had been in the Army two years; now, all of a sudden, he was told to go out and risk his life. He, like most Americans, had never thought of the war in terms of getting killed. In disgust, the second lieutenant said, "All right, sergeant, you just sit here. If any of you bastards," turning to the rest of his men, "have got the guts, follow me. We've got to get that machine gun. A lot of our men are getting killed by that machine gun."

Well, about ten men followed the second lieutenant. They killed the Japs and the machine gun didn't kill any more Americans.

That afternoon the sergeant went to the second lieutenant and said, "Sir, I am ashamed of myself. Give me another chance." By then there was another machine gun to be knocked out. So, the second lieutenant ordered the sergeant to take a squad and knock it out. The sergeant did just that. In fact, he knocked it out personally. The necessity of risking his life had finally been demonstrated to him.

Why didn't the sergeant on Attu do as he was told? Why did he volunteer to do the same thing the second time? I think men fight for two reasons: (1) ideals, (2) *esprit de corps.* The sergeant's education had not included any firm impression of the things that are worth fighting for, so he didn't see why he should risk his life the first time. But the second time he was willing to risk his life for his fellows, for the lieutenant and the ten men who had risked *their* lives, possibly for him, in the morning. The bonds of their common peril of the moment had gripped him as nothing in the past could.

In talking to the Marines aboard the *Blue Fox* I became convinced that they didn't know what to believe in, either—except the Marine Corps. The Marines fought almost solely on *esprit de corps,* I was certain. It was inconceivable to most Marines that they should let another Marine down, or that they could be responsible for dimming the bright reputation of their corps. The Marines simply assumed that they were the world's best fighting men. "Are you afraid?" Bill Hipple asked one of them. "Hell, no, mister," he answered, "I'm a Marine."

There was one man aboard the *Blue Fox* who had made a thorough study of why men fight. Lieutenant Colonel Evans F. Carlson had, during his forty-eight years, seen war in many places. At sixteen he had enlisted in the Army; at twenty-one he was commissioned an officer; in World War I he was a captain in the Adjutant General's department of Pershing's staff. Two years of civilian life convinced him that he was cut out to be a soldier, so he enlisted again, this time as a Marine. After a year as an enlisted man he was commissioned a Marine officer. His most notable tours of duty were with the Marines in China, where he served four times in the next fifteen years. His experience as an observer with the Communist Chinese Eighth Route Army convinced him that social distinctions between officers and enlisted men must be abolished, and that every officer must prove himself before he can command the complete respect of the men in his command. The officer who forgot that his rank was a symbol of great responsibility had no place in Carlson's scheme of things.

Carlson became enthusiastic about the Eighth Army and he became bitter against the Japs the Chinese were fighting. He did not hesitate to say so; therefore, he had to resign from the Marine Corps in 1938. He became a lecturer and an author (*Twin Stars of China* and *The Chinese Army*). He cried out against selling scrap iron to the Japanese. But, after two more years of civilian life, he became convinced that it would be necessary for the United States to go to war. In 1940 he went into the Marines again, this time as a major in the reserves. He was given his finest command, the Second Marine Raider Battalion—Edson had the First—which became known throughout the world as "Carlson's Raiders" after the famed Makin Island raid of August, 1942. At that time the United States needed a spectacular gesture against the Japs. Carlson provided it by bringing his raiders in by submarine and blowing up all Jap installations on Makin. Only two of the one hundred fifty Japs on Makin escaped.

A gaunt, soft-voiced, Lincolnesque sort of man, Carlson ran his Raider Battalion according to the theories that he had been developing for twenty years, the theories that had, he thought, been proved and improved by the Chinese Communists. His officers and men lived and worked together on equal terms—there had to be obedience, of course. The mess cook was made to feel that his job was just as important as the machine gunner's. The battalion adopted as its slogan, *"Gung Ho"* (Work Together). Every man of the 600, chosen out of 7,000, was taught that his life depended on every other man.

"We used to hold discussions," said Colonel Carlson one day when I met him on the *Blue Fox*'s deck. "We would tell these men the implications of the war. We would show the connection between the war in Europe and the war in the Pacific. Then we would ask for questions. It was surprising how those privates could point out things that hadn't occurred to me, and

I had studied global war for a long time. I learned as much from them as they did from me.

"That was a great outfit, that Second Raider Battalion," Carlson said, rubbing his long, sharp chin. "I think they knew what they were fighting for. Anyway, I tried to teach them. We tried to educate them politically—by that I don't mean we told them whom to vote for, but what to believe in. That's harder than teaching them how to shoot a gun. But they learned. Every man knew that if he didn't understand something he had a right as an individual—and we tried to encourage individualism—to ask about it. We made *sure* every man understood all about every operation before we went into battle. It's the only way.

"You spoke about *esprit de corps*. It's mighty important, and the Marine Corps has got it to a high degree. But, when the going gets toughest, when it takes a little bit more drive to keep sane and to keep going, and a man is hungry and tired, then he needs more than *esprit de corps*. It takes conviction.

"That last ounce of sacrifice takes more than *esprit de corps*,

"Our greatest weakness is the caliber of our officers, and that, of course, is a reflection on our system of education. On Guadalcanal, with General Vandegrift's approval, I commissioned sixteen officers in the field. Ex-enlisted men often make the best officers after they have proved themselves in battle. On the other hand, I had to relieve two of my company commanders—it's sometimes hard to tell whether a likely-looking officer will pan out in battle. Then I promoted one of my company commanders to major. This boy—his name was Washburn and he was from Connecticut—crossed over the river, took his company up the shore, then crossed back and came in behind the Japs. They killed seventy of them by surprise. When the Japs collected themselves, Washburn had to withdraw. The Japs thought he had gone. Then Washburn hit them again from five hundred or six hundred yards. He used his head. I promoted him on the spot and it was good for morale, because every man in the company knew that Washburn deserved it."

Ⓞ Colonel Carlson's ideas about indoctrinating soldiers had apparently been passed up by his superiors—the United States military services have never been known for their non-conservatism. The Raider Battalions had all but lost their identity after they were merged into a regiment in 1943. Colonel Carlson was on the Tarawa expedition as an observer for another division, which he served, not as a field commander where he could put his ideas into effect, but as a staff officer. But he, like other observers, was to play an important role on Tarawa.

During the long, sweltering trip to Tarawa the Marines found little excitement. They spent an hour a day cleaning their rifles —the Marine still calls his rifle his best friend—and sharpening their knives and bayonets. Another hour was devoted to studying aerial photographs and twelve-foot contour maps of Betio. Every man concentrated on learning just where he would land and just what he was supposed to do when he got there. A few manned anti-aircraft guns. Besides that there was nothing to do except eat and sleep. They always seemed to be asleep, in their bunks, on the decks, under the landing boats, on any given surface. Some were always playing cards—pitch, gin rummy, solitaire, bridge. Many read dogeared magazines that were anywhere from six weeks to six years old, or pocket-sized Penguin murder mysteries brought up from New Zealand. Every second day there was a new movie of the kind that was usually sent to the armed forces: the kind that was optimistically labeled Grade B by its makers when it was filmed two to five years ago. After witnessing something called *Marry the Boss's Daughter*, a perspiring Marine walked out remarking, "I ought to have my head examined for sitting through that one."

The one consuming passion of the Marines seemed to be letter-writing, as my roommates, the junior officers who had to censor the letters, testified frequently and sometimes profanely. Lieutenant Adolph ("Swede") Norvik, the battalion staff officer charged with mail censorship, spent some eight hours a day reading letters, increased to twelve hours as the ship neared Betio. Finally he had to call on other officers to help, as the mail collector brought in big bags almost hourly and emptied them in the big desk drawers. "I wouldn't mind so much," Norvik cried out, "if that damned corporal didn't write five identical letters to five different girls every day." A high percentage of the letters were addressed to New Zealand, which I reflected might have been food for American isolationists' thought. The Marines could not mention our destination in their letters, or even the fact that we were going into battle—a severe restriction, I thought, since the news of our invasion would have reached all parts of the world weeks before the letters were received. Many times later I pondered on the effect created in many homes where letters were received after the writer had been pronounced "Killed in action." Such was to be the fate of more than a hundred and fifty of the letter writers on the *Blue Fox*.

About halfway between Base X and Tarawa, I attended one of the battalion staff meetings in the wardroom. Presiding officer was the battalion commander, Lieutenant Colonel Herbert R. Amey, Jr., a Pennsylvanian who had moved to San Diego, as had so many Marine officers whose career had become the war. A tall, black-haired, black-mustached officer in his mid-thirties, as handsome as a movie star, Colonel Amey was popular with his staff, his company commanders, and his men. Naturally shy, speechmaking came unnaturally to him, but he had to do it, so he got up and began outlining the plan of battle.

"I'd call these various islands of the Tarawa Atoll by their real names," he said, "but I can't pronounce them. So I'll call them by their code names, which you all know better, anyway. . . . Colonel Shoup's combat team will consist of the three assault battalions, plus detachments of artillery and engineers. Ours is the center battalion, as you know.

"The entire operation depends on our combat team, and we are the center of it. The whole thing hinges on our three battalions. We've got to get that island and the airfield on it. We'll bring in the Seabees and they'll straighten out the air strip and we'll have planes operating off it pretty damn quick. The Navy has always promised us close support and here's where we get it. The land-based bombers start hitting the place D minus four [four days before D Day]. The PBY's will hit Jaluit and Mili to knock out the Jap airfields there. On D minus three a carrier force will hit Tarawa from sun-up to sun-down. D minus two a cruiser force will shell it from sun-up to sun-down. D minus one the carriers hit it again from sun-up to sun-down.

"That's just the beginning. On D Day about dawn the Jap airfields at Nauru, Jaluit, and Mili will be heavily bombed, so there won't be any Jap planes to bother us on Tarawa. On Tarawa itself the air and naval bombardment will be alternated steadily for four hours [here Colonel Amey recited the exact schedule] and they will put a total of about three thousand tons of high explosives on that little square mile in that time. There's never been anything like it. As we hit the beach the planes will be strafing very close in front of you to keep the Nips down until you can get in there and knock off what's left of them. I think we ought to have every Jap off the island—the live ones— by the night of D Day."

Colonel Amey was sweating profusely. I doubt that he had ever made such a long speech before. He continued. "We are very fortunate. This is the first time a landing has been made by American troops against a well-defended beach, the first time over a coral reef, the first time against any force to speak of. And the first time the Japs have had the hell kicked out of them in a hurry.

"Maybe we'll walk ashore. I don't know. It depends on the effect of gunfire and air bombardment."

Lieutenant Norvik got up as Colonel Amey finished. He gave a detailed outline of what we knew about the number of Japs on Tarawa, where they were located, where nearby Jap bases were located and what was based there. The intelligence turned out to be surprisingly accurate—except that we did not know the extraordinary strength of the Jap fortifications. Of the Gilbertese, Norvik said, "They are fine people, very friendly, some speak English. Their heads should never be touched—very important, it has something to do with religion. They are very jealous of their women. There is a native drink made from coconut that makes men insane and want to kill. Natives used to be given six months for possessing it.

"When talking to you the natives may sit down. That's their way of being respectful. The island is very low. Six feet down you hit water, so don't drink it until it has been tested. Dysentery is a big factor—that's why the Japs build their heads [toilets] over the water, which they approach by those little platforms you see in the photographs." Lieutenant Norvik instructed the audience about the password and countersign, and sat down.

Before the meeting broke up, Colonel Amey stood up and shouted, "Just a minute—I forgot a couple of things. Tell your men to drink very little water at first. Every man will take two canteens, but we can't be sure how long it will be before we can get some water ashore. And there will be no pilfering. The M.P.'s will warn you first, then shoot. And don't forget. Hit 'em quick and hit 'em hard. They'll be punchdrunk from the shellfire, so hit 'em before they can pull themselves together."

I was curious to know what various officers thought the effect of the naval gunfire and aerial bombardment would be. Obviously, the ease or difficulty of our task depended on the number of Japs killed or stunned by the preliminary bombing and shelling. When I asked General Julian Smith at Base X, he wouldn't even attempt a guess at first. He finally said he wouldn't count on more than one-third of them being killed before the Marines hit the beach. As indicated above, Colonel Edson was bearish on the effect of the high explosives: "Where the Navy gunnery officers make their mistake is in assuming that land targets are like ships—when you hit a ship it sinks and all is lost, but on land you've got to get direct hits on many installations, and that's impossible, even with three thousand tons of shells and bombs." One day on the *Blue Fox* I went up to see Colonel Shoup and tried to pin him down for an estimate.

"Well," said Dave Shoup, whose "major general's quarters" were the single hottest spot on the transport, "if there are three thousand Nips on the island, I'd say not more than seven hundred will be dead when we get ashore. But the degree of their ability to function will be something else. The bombing and shelling will tear up their communications, for one thing, and they can't fight effectively without communications.

"What worries me more than anything is that our boats may not be able to get over that coral shelf that sticks out about five hundred yards," said Shoup. "We may have to wade in. The first waves, of course, will get in all right on the 'alligators' [amphibious tractors], but if the Higgins boats draw too much water to get in fairly close, we'll either have to wade in with machine guns maybe shooting at us, or the amphtracks will have to run a shuttle service between the beach and the end of the shelf. We have got to calculate high tide pretty closely for the Higgins boats to make it."

I asked a number of enlisted Marines how tough they thought it was going to be. "Tougher than anybody has said," was the consensus. One sergeant went into some detail about his opinion of the Tarawa operation. "We know the Navy is going to hit that damn island with everything there is. But something in the back of my mind tells me there's going to be a lot of shooting Japs left when we start going ashore. What makes me think that? Well, I've seen a lot of bombing and shelling on Tulagi and Guadalcanal, and it never was so awfully effective as these airplane nuts would have you think. Airplanes can sink ships, and they can scare hell out of you on land—I sure don't like to be bombed—but they never actually kill many people. And we've heard about the shelling and bombing of New Georgia—that didn't turn out to be very effective, and our ground troops had a hell of a time, being green like they were. And there was Kiska, which had been bombed and shelled I don't know how many times. But when the Army got ashore they found out it hadn't done much good, even if the Japs had left. The Japs left there because they knew the ground troops were coming, not because of the bombing.

"Now," the sergeant continued, "I know all these things. But at the same time I realize that all the bombing and shelling that has been done in the past, including that in Europe, is child's play compared to what the Nips on Tarawa are going to get. It's hard to imagine three thousand tons of high explosives falling on an island as small as that without killing everything on it, no matter how well the little brown bastards dig in. And, brother, I can testify that they are the damnedest diggers in the world. It's like pulling a tick out of a rug to get one out of his hole. You see what it all adds up to—I don't know what to think, and we won't ever find out until we try it."

I wished I had that sergeant's name. He was the best prophet on the ship. I felt that he was right, at the time. I had left New Guinea after the seventy-second Jap raid on Port Moresby; up to that time not an American on the soil of New Guinea had been killed by Japanese bombing except a few airmen who had been caught in their planes on the ground. And during those raids the Japs had air superiority at almost all times. In those days I liked to console myself by thinking that our bombing was more accurate—it was a year later before I would concede that even the over-publicized Norden bombsight could not kill a Jap when he was in a hole. I had also seen the ineffectiveness of the American bombing on Kiska—the island had barely been touched in the scores of raids between the Japanese occupation in 1942, and the time we landed in August, 1943. Still, three thousand tons on one square mile. . . .

What actually threw me off, and made me unprepared for what we were going to find on Tarawa, was not the preparatory bombing-and-shelling illusion. It was the conversation that took place among the officers during the last two days aboard the *Blue Fox*. One afternoon I wrote in my notebook: "Oh, oh, where have I heard this before? Says Colonel Shoup, 'I don't give a damn if there is not one Jap on the island. Our objective is the airfield, and if we get that without losing a Marine, I'll be happy. Killing every Jap on Tarawa is not worth losing one Marine's life.' "

Dave Shoup continued, "If the Japs meant to trick us into this operation and tie up a big force at the same time, they succeeded. Just look out here"—pointing to the scores of ships extending to the horizon on every side—"battleships, carriers, cruisers, destroyers, and I don't know how many transports and LST's. But we'll put that airfield in operation right away and start bombing the Marshalls."

The cause of this new trend of thought was a report from the B-24's which had bombed Betio the day before: no signs of life on the island, and very weak anti-aircraft fire. Perhaps the Japs were pulling out, just as they had pulled out of Kiska. That phrase, "Very weak anti-aircraft fire," had such a familiar ring! The night in August before our convoy sailed from Adak for Kiska I had talked with the B-25 pilots who had bombed Kiska twice that day. Said one of the senior pilots, Major Richard Salter, "I don't believe there are any Japs on Kiska. I haven't seen a sign of movement in two weeks of bombing the island. The new pilots come back and report 'Very weak anti-aircraft fire,' but new pilots are always seeing things. There isn't any anti-aircraft fire at all."

Thus, I edged myself into thinking that the Japs had left Tarawa, too. I knew it was a dangerous frame of mind for someone going in with the assault waves, and I noted the feeling in my book. "If there are a lot of Japs on Tarawa I'll be utterly unprepared psychologically." The feeling among the officers increased as we neared Tarawa. "The chances are fifty-fifty this is another Kiska," one artillery officer offered to bet, without finding any takers. A transport surgeon who had also gone through the Kiska dry-run was caustic: "There won't be a damned Jap on Tarawa, and I'll bet we haven't got an alternate target. Why in the hell don't we just take this force and keep going to Tokyo and get the goddam war over with?" he said, knowing nothing about the difficulty of supply and organization and the millions of gallons of oil such a force needed for only one day's steaming.

Try as I might, I never got over the feeling that the Japs had pulled out of Tarawa—not until the first bullet whizzed by my ear.

There were three chaplains on board the *Blue Fox:* the Protestant, M. J. MacQueen, the Catholic, F. W. Kelly, who were attached to the Marines, and the ship's chaplain, Peter R. McPhee, Jr. As the ship neared the target their duties increased progressively. If there was any sign of nervousness or fear or intimation of approaching fate, the Marines showed it in their increasing attention to religion. This is, of course, as it should be. In battle death is as normal as life, and any man is a fool who goes into battle without adjusting himself to admit, "I may be killed," and steeling himself to say, "I am not afraid to die." The man who is prepared to die, should that be his lot, approaches battle calmer and with a clearer head. He is a better soldier.

Religious services were usually held on deck. Several times daily the ship's loudspeaker would drone: "Protestant services will be held at 1700 on Number Seven hatch," or "Catholic mass is now being held on Number Four hatch." Father Kelly was a young, black-haired, blue-eyed priest from Upper Darby, Pennsylvania, who was frequently asked in friendly fashion by Marines from the Protestant South whether he was married. About twenty-seven percent of the men of the battalion were Catholics, but Father Kelly was as popular with the Protestants, just as Chaplain MacQueen was as popular with the Catholics as with the Protestants. Denominational distinctions did not mean much to men about to offer up their lives.

"This is probably the most informal type of service in the

world," said Father Kelly. "I hold mass on deck, and I hold confession in a corner of the wardroom. The boys come and tell me
what they have done, say they are sorry, and that's that." Later,
on Betio, I was to see Chaplain Kelly supervising the burial of
many of these men who had made their last confession to him
not many hours before. Amid the buoyancy of life or the still-
ness of death, Chaplain Kelly, like the Marines who were his
charges, was a professional.

Of all the Marines on the *Blue Fox*, there were none more
professional than the thirty-four men of the regimental Scout
and Sniper Platoon. This platoon had been formed of picked
men after the Second Regiment had found the need for some
such group of experts on Guadalcanal; qualifications for the
S. & S. platoon included not only the dead-eye of an expert rifleman and the patience of an Indian—the heart of absolute fear-
lessness was just as important. All the Marines, it seemed, hated
the Japs. Said Colonel Shoup, "The New Zealanders used to ask
me how we instilled such bitter hatred in our men. I said we
didn't instill it. 'Just wait until you see a lot of your buddies
shot to pieces by the Japs,' I said. And you get mad at 'em for
making life so miserable and uncomfortable. We wouldn't be
out in these stinking jungles if the Japs hadn't attacked us." But
there were no Marines who hated the Japs more than the Scout
and Sniper men. Through bitter experience they had learned
that men who hate most, kill best. "I just want to kill them all—
that's all," said a Polish-American private first-class.

Except that they were all picked troops and they knew they
were élite of the élite Marines, the Scout-Sniper men had not
very much in common. The thirty-four men came from eighteen
different states—five from Wisconsin, five from California. Their
racial background was a ladleful from the American melting
pot: Gunnery Sergeant Hooper, the second in command, was
from Milford, New Jersey; there were Davis from Tennessee,
Gillis from Ipswich, Massachusetts, Deka and Krzys from Cleve-

land, Leseman and Kloskowski from Wisconsin, Selavka from Connecticut and Allred from Sophia, North Carolina, Putz from Forest Hills, New York, and Collins from Chatham, New York. Besides Hooper, there were three other sergeants, nine corporals; the rest were privates first-class.

The rest, that is, except the platoon's leader: First Lieutenant William D. Hawkins of El Paso. I saw "Hawk," as everybody called him, several times on the *Blue Fox*. The last time I saw him was the day before D Day. We stood topside after dinner, watching the miracle of the equatorial sunset: gold and flaming red, slate-gray and solid blue streaks and green streaks. To the west, between our ship and the sunset the outlines grew dimmer, as the sun set lower, of some forty American ships of war. Hawkins was saying, "You know, we're going in first. We are going to wipe every last one of the bastards off that pier and out from under that pier before they have a chance to pick off the first wave. But one man had to stay behind to take care of our equipment. I asked for volunteers. Not a man in the crowd would volunteer to stay behind. My men are not afraid of danger."

The first time I had met Hawkins he had said, quite calmly, as though he were telling me what time it was, "I think the thirty-four men in my platoon can lick any two-hundred-man company in the world."

After his death, and after Julian Smith had named the airfield on Betio after him, I learned more about this twenty-nine-year-old Texan, who was, I thought, the bravest man I have ever known.

William Deane Hawkins was born April 19, 1914, in Fort Scott, Kansas. His father was from Louisiana and his mother was the daughter of a Missouri doctor. When he was three years old, and his family was living in Los Angeles, the most important event of his life occurred: a neighbor, using the Hawkins kitchen to do her washing, walked out a door holding a pan of scalding water; little Deane Hawkins ran into her and upset the pan. He suffered severe burns on a third of the surface of his body—his arms, his back, a shoulder, a leg. One leg was drawn and an arm was crooked so that he could not straighten it. The doctors wanted to cut the muscles, but Deane Hawkins' mother was not sure. For a year she massaged her little boy's arm and leg daily for two or three hours. Finally, to the amazement of the doctors, the muscles lived again. At the end of a year Deane Hawkins, cured, was learning again to walk.

When he was five the Hawkinses were again living in Kansas. En route to Phoenix, they stopped in El Paso, where his father, an insurance-claim adjuster, was persuaded to settle. When Deane Hawkins was eight his father died. His mother went to work, first as secretary to the high-school principal, then as a teacher of commercial subjects in El Paso Technical Institute.

Deane Hawkins' scars were always with him. By the time he was ten he was a fine swimmer, but one day he came home from the Y. M. C. A. unhappy and brooding. "Aw, mom," he said, "I don't think I'm going to the Y any more. When I take off my clothes the kids all look and say, 'Oh, look at Deane!'" His mother reassured him. "Son, it's not your fault; you have nothing to be ashamed of." He went back to the Y swimming pool.

He wanted to get into the Navy, to study aeronautical engineering; he had plane models with "doped" cloth fuselages and rubber-band power plants flying all over the house. But he had no influence; he knew no congressman who would appoint him to the Naval Academy. So he persuaded two friends, James Colley, later of the Marines, and William Abbott, later a naval pilot, to enlist with him with a view to taking the sailors' merit examination for Annapolis. The two friends got into the Navy. But Deane Hawkins did not; he had scars. Said the recruiting officer, "I never hated to turn down anyone so much in all my life. You're the kind of boy the Navy wants." Deane Hawkins went home to his mother. "They made it," he sobbed. "It was my idea and I didn't."

The scars were to haunt him still further. When he was

eighteen he had a railroad job. He was working under a car when an engine humped it. In scrambling from beneath the car he dislocated a vertebra. When he took a physical examination before returning to work the railroad doctor saw the scars and said, "Nothing doing; you are not a good risk." Later he tried to enlist as a cadet flyer in the Army Air Forces. The scars kept him out.

Deane Hawkins was a smart boy—at El Paso's Lamar and Alta Vista Schools and at El Paso High School. He skipped the fifth grade. He won the state chemistry-essay contest, graduated from high school at sixteen, and was awarded a scholarship to the Texas College of Mines, where he studied engineering. Like most sons of the poor, he worked. After school and during summer vacation he sold magazines and delivered newspapers; he was a bank messenger and he made photostats for an abstract company. He was a ranchhand, a railroad hand, and a bellhop. At seventeen when he was skinny and six feet tall he met a hotel guest who told him laborers were needed to lay a pipeline in New Mexico. Deane Hawkins went to New Mexico, where the hiring boss laughed at him. "Sonny, two-hundred-pound men are collapsing on this job." But he gave the kid a chance, and Deane Hawkins worked twelve hours a day lifting, with the help of one full-grown man, four-hundred-pound creosoted pipe. When his mother saw her son a week later, she was horrified at the skinny boy, burned by wind, sun, sand, and creosote. "I'm all right now, mom," he said, "but the first day I thought I'd die."

Deane Hawkins was quiet and serious. He liked to go dancing, but he had no use for jitterbugs. He didn't like a certain girl because "She can't carry on a sensible conversation; she giggles too much." Sometimes he took his mother to a dance. He helped her to make the beds, sweep the floors, and he could cook. When he had enough money he bought a car—not a jalopy, but a conservative blue Ford roadster.

He left home when he was twenty-one. He worked two and

a half years in Tacoma, Washington, in a dank, underground office so unlike the Texas outdoors. He was married there, and divorced. Then he went to work as an engineer for a Los Angeles title-insurance company. He was there when Pearl Harbor happened. Before the war he had said, "I hate war. I don't see why the United States ought to get in it." But when the United States was forced into it, Deane Hawkins said, "I've got to go. I'm going to see if the Marines will have me." That was when he was at home, at Christmas, 1941. There was no Marine recruiting office in El Paso, so he went back to Los Angeles to enlist. He was very proud when "the toughest outfit of them all" accepted him, scars and all.

"Hawk" was what all the Marines called him, in boot camp, in commando school, in battle—when he was killed, nobody from his own outfit could remember his first name. When his regiment went overseas in June, 1942, Hawkins was a private first-class. On shipboard he was promoted to corporal; by the time he landed on Tulagi in August, he was a sergeant, and before the Battle of the Solomons was a month old he had been commissioned a second lieutenant. Wrote a Marine sergeant to his mother, "When he was a sergeant, I knew he would make a fine officer. . . . Your son was born to lead and I would have followed him anywhere. . . . You see, 'Hawk' loved trouble. If there was a tough job to do, he'd ask for it."

He sent his mother high-spirited, amusing letters from Tulagi and Guadalcanal. "I heard the darnedest argument last night. I woke up and was being carried into the jungle by two bugs. I heard one bug say, 'Shall we eat him here, or carry him a little farther?' And the other bug said, 'Hell, no, let's eat him here before some big bug comes along and takes him away from us.' "

Like handsome Deane Hawkins himself, his friends were orderly youngsters: Ballard McClesky, Wallace Love, and Austin Pritchett. They all, like tens of thousands of liberty-loving Texans, left good jobs to volunteer in the armed services. Earlier they, like Hawkins, had worked after school to supplement family incomes. After Deane Hawkins's death, Sergeant Mc-Clesky of the U. S. Army wrote to Deane Hawkins's mother: "Mom, did I ever tell you of the last talk Deane and I had the Christmas of 1941 when we were together? With Pearl Harbor only a short time before and Deane's plans to enter the Marines completed, we naturally spoke of the future that we could expect. Deane's last words to me were: 'Mac, I'll see you someday, but not on this earth.' Even before he left, he knew he wasn't coming back."

After I had returned from Tarawa, Mrs. Hawkins wrote to me, as so many mothers, fathers, and wives write to war correspondents, a letter of great dignity, asking if I could tell her the details of her son's death. "Those things mean so much to me," she said. "He was my whole world, all I had. . . . He lived as he died, always on the peak of excellence. He was a wonderful son, always cheerful, confident, sweet, kind, and thoughtful of others. . . . Please help me, if you can, to get a complete picture of his last days. . . . I hope I am not imposing when I ask you to do this for me."

I wrote Mrs. Hawkins all that I could recall of Hawk. Then I added a last paragraph. "I do not know what else I can say. What can one say about a man who died so nobly in the service of his country? If Lieutenant Hawkins had lived a hundred years, he could not have known a fuller life. He could not have achieved more. Hawk knew what the war was about. He knew that we must crush the Japanese utterly, so that our sons will not have this war to fight again in twenty or thirty years hence. His example of devotion and unselfishness will surely serve to sustain other millions of young men who must finish the job. His name will live always in the brightest pages of those men who are proud to call themselves 'United States Marines.' "

On the day before the battle there came to the men aboard the *Blue Fox* a mimeographed message:

"To the officers and men of the Second Division:

"A great offensive to destroy the enemy in the Central Pacific has begun. American air, sea and land forces, of which this division is a part, initiate this offensive by seizing Japanese-held atolls in the Gilbert Islands which will be used as bases for future operations. The task assigned to us is to capture the atolls of Tarawa and Abemama. Army units of our own Fifth Amphibious Corps are simultaneously attacking Makin, 105 miles north of Tarawa. . . .

"Our Navy screens our operations and will support our attack tomorrow with the greatest concentration of aerial bombardment and naval gunfire in the history of warfare. It will remain with us until our objective is secured and our defenses are established. Garrison troops are already en route to relieve us as soon as we have completed our job of clearing our objective of Japanese forces.

"This division was especially chosen by the high command for the assault on Tarawa because of its battle experience and its combat efficiency. Their confidence in us will not be betrayed. We are the first American troops to attack a defended atoll. . . . Our people back home are eagerly awaiting news of our victories.

"I know that you are well-trained and fit for the tasks assigned to you. You will quickly overrun the Japanese forces; you will decisively defeat and destroy the treacherous enemies of our country. Your success will add new laurels to the glorious traditions of our Corps.

"Good luck and God bless you all,

JULIAN C. SMITH,
*Major General, U. S. Marine Corps
Commanding"*

This day before the battle probably deserves some detailing. It was hot, as all days en route to Tarawa were hot. There was a slightly increased tension among the Marines—nothing exciting, just a sort of stretching and unlimbering, as men who are about to undertake something flex themselves. They made up their rolls which would follow them ashore: blankets and shelter halves and mess gear; beyond their weapons these assault troops themselves would take nothing with them except ammunition, water canteens, a day's emergency rations—C and K— and a spotted poncho for light cover. A dozen at a time would gather in the wardroom to study intently the big table-mounted relief map of Betio, which was detailed to the point of glued-on miniature palm trees.

The Marines cleaned their rifles for the last time, applying oil industriously with small paint brushes, lovingly stroking the barrel as they removed the last tiny grain of dirt with a ramrod into whose slit a folded circular piece of cloth had been inserted. They wrote their final letters—which Swede Norvik censored, though he had sent out a notice two days previously that the mails were closed. They joked with one another. "Hey, Bill," said one Marine to another, "I just remembered I still owe you a pack of cigarettes. I want to pay you before we get killed. Say, you want to buy a good watch?" Said Bill, "We'll get that watch off you on the way back."

At 1310 (1:10 P.M.) came the thumping buzz (twenty-three buzzes) for General Quarters, which meant that we might expect an attack from the enemy at any time. I lay in my bunk, reading *Deadline* by the French newspaperman, Pierre Lazareff, growing angrier as I read, because the French had been stupid enough to be misled into apathy or comradeship toward the Germans. Gamelin, Bonnet, Laval, Daladier. For these names I had no difficulty in substituting Lindbergh, Nye, Wheeler, McCormick, but it was consoling to recall that these blind Americans had not held correspondingly important positions in the United States Government during our critical moments. And Congress had voted for Lend-Lease despite Lindbergh's testimony in January, 1941, to the effect that Germany, with her overpowering technological superiority, was a sure bet to win,

and "the position of Great Britain becomes more and more difficult." I remembered Lindbergh's appearance before the House
Foreign Affairs Committee under the sponsorship of a congressman named Fish in the resplendent new House Office Building's
committee room. To me he had seemed at the time a guileless,
bewildered young man who had been sold a bill of goods by
Goering, a man trying to buck the inevitable—like honest-
intentioned young Bob LaFollette—because his father had
bucked it in the dim past of 1917. Now, as General Quarters
sounded on the day before the Tarawa battle, Lindbergh seemed
in retrospect, not a traitor—only a young "colonel" who had
never been in battle.

These thoughts were interrupted by the ship's loudspeaker.
"This is no drill!" Theretofore, on the *Blue Fox,* General
Quarters had meant only a rehearsal for the appearance of real
enemy submarines or real enemy planes. Reluctantly I put on a
steel helmet and snapped a rubber lifebelt around my waist and
went topside. There were perhaps a hundred planes in the
bright sunlight around us, but no sign of the expected enemy.

"It's a wonderful feeling," said Colonel Carlson. "Many
planes and they are all ours." I asked him what the scoop was—
"scoop" is the Marine word for Army "dope" and Navy "scuttle-
butt." "Don't know a thing," he said, "except the order was
'Prepare to repel air attack.' " Unless one stands on the bridge
beside the captain, news travels slowly on board ship. It was ten
hours later that I learned from the young Michigan major,
Howard Rice, that it was far-ranging friendly planes which had
caused the alert.

After an hour on deck, watching the bright, pale-blue sky, un-
mottled except for a few wisps of white clouds near the horizon,
I heard the "secure from General Quarters" signal and went below again. In the passageway I met Father Kelly and asked if the
word about "another Kiska" had reached the Marines. "Some of
them have heard that there may not be any Japs on Tarawa," he
said, "and you know what their reaction is? They hope there are

at least *some* Japs left there. They say they would hate to come all this way for nothing."

The night before the battle was upside-down. The enlisted men were to start eating "breakfast" at 10 P.M., the officers at midnight. The menu was steak and eggs, a British dish which the Marines during their long New Zealand stay had come to favor over the American ham and eggs. "Jesus," said one of the transport surgeons, "that will make a nice lot of guts to have to sew up—full of steak." In the U. S. armed forces, it occurred to me, steak had become the standard menu on the night before D Day—in the Army, the Navy, and the Marine Corps, the Government seemed to stand up and say, "You men, you who are about to go into battle, you are our foundation; without you young men we would not exist; you are our better physical specimens, none of you is 4-F. Therefore, I, the Government, want you to have the best food we've got. I know you had your weekly meal of steak only last night, but I want you to go into battle knowing that I gave you the best meal I could."

Catholic mass was held in the wardroom at 1900. Physically, it was oppressive. Some five hundred men knelt in the dripping room or in the passageways leading to the room—it was built to seat about two hundred maximum. The heat and the stench from the bodies of so many sweltering men hit one in the face like a bucket of dishwater, even from a distance down the corridor. I never got to know what Father Kelly said in his last prayer to steel the men who were about to die.

I went back to the junior staff officers' bunkroom. I took down my helmet and put in it a folded sheaf of toilet paper and a jungle-green mosquito head-net. In the pockets of my green Marine Corps dungarees I put a can of C ration and a pack of K ration. I filled my two canteens with fresh water. One of the transport surgeons gave me two morphine syrettes and a two-ounce bottle of medicinal brandy. I got out two fresh notebooks —if I were killed I did not want the Japs to learn anything about us from the notes I had made during the convoy trip. My barracks bag, which contained all my clothing except what I wore, and my typewriter, I left to be brought ashore at some indefinite date—when the island was ours.

Three and a half hours before midnight we turned out the light in our bunkroom and tried to sleep. I had convinced myself, to my own detriment, that all the Japs had left Tarawa, that we were in for another Kiska. The idea fairly obsessed me. I should have slept, but I did not. Instead, I leaned over every half hour, reached for a cigarette and hoped that my lighting it did not wake up my roommates. I need not have worried. When we were called at ten minutes before midnight, we all observed that we had been as wide-awake as a two-months-old baby yelling for his six-o'clock bottle. That is, all except the red-headed boy from Athens, Texas, Marine Gunner Stogner, who had already broken all records for sleeping. For the rest of us the excitement of possibly landing in the face of hostile enemy fire was too much. We all half believed, and I nine-tenths believed, that the Japs would be gone. But there was the possibility. . . .

THE FIRST DAY

WE JUMPED OUT of bed at midnight, swimming in sweat. We donned our dungarees and headed for the wardroom. Nobody took more than fifteen minutes to eat his steak, eggs, and fried potatoes and drink his two cups of coffee, but everybody was soaking before he had finished. This was the hottest night of all. Before we filed out, gasping, there was an oversupply of the rumors that attend every battle: one of our cruisers had sunk a Jap surface craft (though not until seventy-seven six-inch shells had been fired, and an accompanying destroyer had let go two torpedoes); one of our ships had been attacked by a Japanese bomber during the night; a searchlight off Betio had already tried to spot our force.

After making last-minute adjustments of my gear, I went up on the flying bridge when General Quarters was buzzed at 0215. There was a half-moon dodging in and out of the clouds forty-five degrees to portside. It was cool up there, with a brisk breeze on the rise. It was possible to make notes when the moon was out. A calm voice came over the loudspeaker: "Target at 112 true, 26,800 yards ahead." "*Blackfish* 870 yards." "*Blackfish* 1000 yards." "*Blackfish* 900 yards." The *Blackfish* was the lead transport, and the *Blue Fox* was next. The faint red signal light of the lead ship slowly flashed on and off as we followed her to Tarawa.

Lieutenant Vanderpoel, the ship's gunnery officer, was talking to me and Lieutenant Commander Fabian, who was to be beach-master on Tarawa. Vanderpoel was indignant. He had seen a lot of this war, at Guadalcanal, Tulagi, Attu, Kiska. And they had never allowed him to fire his guns on the transport. True, they were not heavy guns such as battleships carry, but they might help. If he could just turn them on the shore, as the warships would turn theirs. "Just once I want to shoot," he said, "but this time they said again 'Transports will not fire.' We sit on these damn transports and we don't get to see anything of the war, and the Marines have to go in and do it all. Damn."

By 0330 the Marines had begun loading the outboard boats for the first wave. The sergeants were calling the roll: "Vernon, Simms, Gresholm. . . ." They needed no light to call the well-remembered roll, and they didn't have to send a runner to find any absentees. The Marines were all there. One of the sergeants was giving his men last-minute instructions: "Be sure to correct your elevation and windage. Adjust your sights."

At 0400 I went below. I stood outside the wardroom as the first and second waves walked through and out to their boats. Most of the men were soaked; their green-and-brown-spotted jungle dungarees had turned a darker green when the sweat from their bodies soaked through. They jested with one another. Only a few even whistled to keep up their courage.

"How many you going to kill, Bunky?" one of them shouted at a bespectacled Marine. "All I can get," said Bunky, without smiling, as he wiped his beloved rifle barrel.

"Oh, boy," said a kid well under twenty, "I just want to spit in a dead Jap's face. Just open his mouth and let him have it."

Said another, "I should have joined the Boy Scouts. I knew it."

They were a grimy, unshaven lot. The order had gone out: they must put on clean clothing just before going ashore, in order to diminish the chances of infection from wounds, but now they looked dirty. Under the weight, light though it was, of their combat packs, lifebelts, guns, ammunition, helmets, canvas leggings, bayonets, they were sweating in great profusion. Nobody had shaved for two or three days.

Outside I saw Dr. Edwin J. Welte, a crop-haired, young Minnesotan who had finished medical school only about five years ago. "Well," he said, "nobody is trying to get out of fighting this battle. Out of the whole battalion only eleven are being left in the ship's sick bay. Five are recurring malaria cases, one busted his knee on maneuvers, one is a post-operative appendectomy, one is a chronic knee that somebody palmed off on the regiment, and the rest are minor shipboard accidents. All the malaria cases will be able to go ashore in two days."

Who else was being left behind? "Nobody that I know of except one pfc. who got obstreperous and they had to throw him in the brig. Only one man in the brig the whole trip, and he's always been a bad character."

We walked back to the junior staff officers' bunkroom, which was full of young Marines indulging in what might have been a college bull session. Outside we could hear the dynamo-hum of the cables letting the boats down into the water. Everybody had on his pack and his helmet, for all these men were going on the assault waves which would start leaving for Betio in ten or fifteen minutes. Young, mustachioed Captain Ben Owens, the Oklahoma boy who was battalion operations officer, looked up as we entered, and said, "Doc, I'm going to get shot in the tail today."

Dr. Welte: "Oh, you want a Purple Heart, huh?"

Owens: "Hell, no, I want a stateside * ticket."

Colonel Amey, the battalion boss, came in, stretched mightily, and ho-hummed. I asked him how many Japs we were going to find on Betio. "Not many, apparently," he said. "They've got five-inch guns. They'd have been shooting at us by now."

_____
* "Stateside," meaning "back to the United States," is a Marine term.

Owens looked at the deck a minute and said, "That's right. We're only eleven thousand yards offshore now. They've got some eight-inch guns, too. But just wait. You'll hear one whistle over in a minute. When he does those battlewagons will open up on that son-of-a-bitch and rock that island——"

Owens continued, "Maybe the battlewagons and the bombs will knock out the big guns, but I'm not saying they'll kill all the Japs. I still think we'll get shot at when we go in, and I'm still looking for that stateside ticket, Doc."

Jay Odell, a slender young junior-grade lieutenant who learned how to be a naval air-liaison officer after leaving his Philadelphia newspaper job, had been standing in a corner without saying anything. Now he spoke up, "Everybody is putting too much faith in the statistics about the number of tons that's going to be dropped."

Now, at 0505, we heard a great thud in the southwest. We knew what that meant. The first battleship had fired the first shot. We all rushed out on deck. The show had begun. The show for which thousands of men had spent months of training, scores of ships had sailed thousands of miles, for which Chaplains Kelly and MacQueen had offered their prayers. The curtain was up in the theatre of death.

We were watching when the battleship's second shell left the muzzle of its great gun, headed for Betio. There was a brilliant flash in the darkness of the half-moonlit night. Then a flaming torch arched high into the air and sailed far away, slowly, very slowly, like an easily lobbed tennis ball. The red cinder was nearly halfway to its mark before we heard the thud, a dull roar as if some mythological giant had struck a drum as big as Mount Olympus. There was no sign of an explosion on the unseen island—the second shot had apparently fallen into the water, like the first.

Within three minutes the sky was filled again with the orange-red flash of the big gun, and Olympus boomed again. The red ball of fire that was the high-explosive shell was again dropping toward the horizon. But this time there was a tremendous burst on the land that was Betio. A wall of flame shot five hundred feet into the air, and there was another terrifying explosion as the shell found its mark. Hundreds of the awestruck Marines on the deck of the *Blue Fox* cheered in uncontrollable joy. Our guns had found the enemy. Probably the enemy's big eight-inch guns and their powder magazine on the southwest corner of the island.

Now that we had the range the battleship sought no longer. The next flash was four times as great, and the sky turned a brighter, redder orange, greater than any flash of lightning the Marines had ever seen. Now four shells, weighing more than a ton each, peppered the island. Now Betio began to glow brightly from the fires the bombardment pattern had started.

That was only the beginning. Another battleship took up the firing—four mighty shells poured from its big guns onto another part of the island. Then another battleship breathed its brilliant breath of death. Now a heavy cruiser let go with its eight-inch guns, and several light cruisers opened with their fast-firing six-inch guns. They were followed by the destroyers, many destroyers with many five-inch guns on each, firing almost as fast as machine guns. The sky at times was brighter than noontime on the equator. The arching, glowing cinders that were high-explosive shells sailed through the air as though buckshot were being fired out of many shotguns from all sides of the island. The Marines aboard the *Blue Fox* exulted with each blast on the island. Fire and smoke and sand obscured the island of Betio. Now the Jap, the miserable, little brown man who had started this horrible war against a peace-loving people, was beginning to suffer the consequences. He had asked for this, and he should have known it before he flew into Pearl Harbor that placid Sunday morning. As the warships edged in closer, coming into shore from many thousands of yards until they were only a few thousand yards away from their target, the whole island of Betio seemed to erupt with bright fires that were burn-

ing everywhere. They blazed even through the thick wall of
smoke that curtained the island.

The first streaks of dawn crept through the sky. The warships continued to fire. All of a sudden they stopped. But here
came the planes—not just a few planes: a dozen, a score, a hundred. The first torpedo bombers raced across the smoking con-
flagration and loosed their big bombs on an island that must
have been dead a half hour ago! They were followed by the dive
bombers, the old workhorse SBD's and the new Helldivers, the
fast SB2C's that had been more than two years a-borning. The
dive bombers lined up, many of thousands of feet over Betio,
then they pointed their noses down and dived singly, or in pairs
or in threes. Near the end of their dives they hatched the bombs
from beneath their bellies; they pulled out gracefully and
sailed back to their carriers to get more bombs. Now came the
fighter planes, the fast, new Grumman Hellcats, the best planes
ever to squat on a carrier. They made their runs just above the
awful, gushing pall of smoke, their machine guns spitting hundreds of fifty-caliber bullets a minute.

Surely, we all thought, no mortal men could live through
such destroying power.

Surely, I thought, if there were actually any Japs left on the
island (which I doubted strongly), they would all be dead by
now.

It was a half hour after dawn that I got a first rude
shock. A shell splashed into the water not thirty feet from an
LST which waited near the *Blue Fox*. Our destroyers, which by
this time were firing again as the planes finished their bombing
and strafing runs, were firing very wide, I surmised. A shell hit
not more than fifty yards from our stern, sending a vertical
stream of water high into the air, like a picture of a geyser
erupting.

I turned to Major Howard Rice and said, "My God, what
wide shooting! Those boys need some practice."

Major Rice looked at me quizzically. Said he, "You don't think that's our own guns doing *that* shooting, do you?"

Then, for the first time, I realized that there were some Japs on Betio. Like a man who has swallowed a piece of steak without chewing it, I said, "Oh."

By this time our first three waves of boats were already in the water, and the fourth and fifth were getting ready to load. But the sudden appearance of the enemy upset our plans. These valuable transports, with their thousands of troops, could not stand idly by and take a chance on being sunk. By now we were within four or five miles of the target. We had no definite knowledge that all the Japs' big guns on Betio were not still working. Captain John McGovern, commodore of the assault transport division, gave the order. The transports heeled around quickly and set out to sea, whence we had come only two hours ago.

The transports streaked out of the danger zone, with the Japs firing vainly at them as they went. The first three waves, including hundreds of boats from many transports, had no choice but to turn around and streak after the mother ships. As they turned and ran our warships opened up again. By firing his gun the Jap had given away its location. Now the fury of the warships, big and small, mounted into a crescendo of unprecedented fire and thunder. They pounded the Jap with everything in the gunnery officer's book. If there had been an unearthly flash of lightning before daylight, now, at close range, there was a nether world of pandemonium. Hundreds of shells crashed with hundreds of ear-rocking thuds as they poured toward the Jap big-gun position. Soon there was no more firing. The last Jap big gun had been silenced. Now the transports could finish loading their assault waves into the boats, and Betio would soon feel the tread of the U. S. Marines' boondockers.*

The fifth wave climbed down the rope nets at 0635, into the

* Marine shoes with thick soles and soft, rough leather tops.

landing boats which bobbed drunkenly on the rough sea and smacked into the transport. Within five minutes after we pushed off, a half barrel of water was splashing over the high bow of the Higgins boat every minute. Every one of the thirty-odd men was soaked before we had chugged a half mile. While a Marine held his poncho over our heads I tried to put my fine watch into a small, heavy waterproof envelope. It seemed a pity to lose such a watch, especially since Sergeant Neil Shober, a craftsman with a jeep or with a strip of metal, had made a handsome wristband for the watch out of a piece of Jap Zero wing he had brought from Guadalcanal. Into another envelope I dropped my newly filled cigarette lighter and some valuable pictures; into another a pack of cigarettes.

The sun had hardly leaped above the horizon and we shivered as the cool seawater drenched us, it seemed, beyond the saturation point. I remembered the nip of brandy the doctor had given me. I pulled the little bottle out of my pocket and shared it with the Marine standing next to me. If there was ever an occasion for taking a drink at seven o'clock in the morning this was it.

Later that day I was to tremble all over from fear alone, but not yet. We shook and shivered because we were cold. My only memory of the first hour and a half of the ride toward the beachhead is sheer discomfort, alternating with exaltation. Our warships and planes were now pounding the little island of Betio as no other island had been pounded in the history of warfare. By standing on the gunwale of the boat I could crane my neck around the ramp-bow and see the smoke and dust and flames of Betio. When the attack paused a moment I could see the palm trees outlined against the sea and sky on the other side.

Once I tried to count the number of salvos—not shells, salvos —the battleships, cruisers, and destroyers were pouring on the island. A Marine who had a waterproof watch offered to count off the seconds up to one minute. Long before the minute had ended I had counted over one hundred, but then a dozen more ships opened up and I abandoned the project. I did count the number of planes in sight at one time. It was ninety-two. These ships and these planes were dealing out an unmerciful beating on the Japs, and it was good, good to watch. As we came within two miles of the island we could get a better view of what was happening. There were fires up and down the length of the island. Most of them would be the barracks, the power plant, the kitchens, and other above-ground installations we had studied time and again in the photographs. Once in a while a solid mass of flame would reach for the sky and the roar of an explosion could be heard easily from our position in the water. That would be an oil tank or an ammunition dump. The feeling was good.

It was nearly nine o'clock when the fifth wave arrived at the boat rendezvous and began circling to wait for our turn to go in. I looked around the ramp to see what was on the beach. For the first time I felt that something was wrong. The first waves were not hitting the beach as they should. There were very few boats on the beach, and these were all amphibious tractors which the first wave used. There were no Higgins boats on the beach, as there should have been by now.

Almost before we could guess at what bad news was being foretold the command boat came alongside. The naval officer shouted, "You'll have to go in right away, as soon as I can get an amphtrack for you. The shelf around the island is too shallow to take the Higgins boats." This was indeed chilling news. It meant something that had been dimly foreseen but hardly expected: the only way the Marines were going to land was in the amphtracks ("alligators") which could crawl over the shallow reef that surrounds Betio. It meant that the landings would be slow, because there were not enough amphtracks for everybody, and we would have to use the emergency shuttle system that had been worked out as a last resort. And suppose the amphtracks were knocked out before they could get enough men ashore to hold what the first wave had taken? And suppose the

Marines already ashore were killed faster than they could be replaced under this slow shuttle system?

I felt very dull—a brain fed on the almost positive belief that the Japs had fled Betio would naturally be slower than a six-year-old writing a letter. I could not quite comprehend what was happening.

An amphtrack bobbed alongside our Higgins boat. Said the Marine amphtrack boss, "Quick! Half you men get in here. They need help bad on the beach. A lot of Marines have already been killed and wounded." While the amphtrack was alongside, Jap shells from an .automatic weapon began peppering the water around us. "Probably a 40-mm.," said one of the calmer Marine officers.

But the Marines did not hesitate. Hadn't they been told that other Marines "needed help bad"? Major Rice and seventeen others scampered into the amphtrack and headed for the beach. I did not see them again until three days later, when the battle was over.

The half-empty Higgins boat milled around for another ten minutes, getting its share of near misses and air bursts. One Marine picked a half dozen pieces of shrapnel off his lap and swallowed hard. Two amphtracks came by. One of our Marines stood up and waved at them, told them that we were ready and waiting to go to the beach. But both had already been disabled by direct hits. Both had wounded and dead men in them, the drivers said. We milled around another couple of minutes, looking for a chance at what appeared to be a one-way ride, but always remembering that "they need help bad" on the beach.

The next amphtrack crew said they would take us in part of the way, to where we could wade the rest of the way, but amphtracks were getting so scarce he couldn't take us all the way. We jumped into the little tractor boat and quickly settled on the deck. "Oh, God, I'm scared," said the little Marine, a telephone operator, who sat next to me forward in the boat. I gritted my teeth and tried to force a smile that would not come and tried to stop quivering all over (now I was shaking from fear). I said, in an effort to be reassuring, "I'm scared, too." I never made a more truthful statement in all my life. I was not petrified yet, but my joints seemed to be stiffening.

Now, I realized, this is the payoff. Now I knew, positively, that there were Japs, and evidently plenty of them, on the island. They were not dead. The bursts of shellfire all around us evidenced the fact that there was plenty of life in them. "This is not going to be a new kind of beachhead landing," I said to myself. "This is going to be traditional—what you have always been told is the toughest of all military operations: a landing, if possible, in the face of enemy machine guns that can mow men down by the hundreds." This was not even going to be the fifth wave. After the first wave there apparently had not been any organized waves, those organized waves which hit the beach so beautifully in the last rehearsal. There had been only an occasional amphtrack which hit the beach, then turned around (if it wasn't knocked out) and went back for more men. There we were: a single boat, a little wavelet of our own, and we were already getting the hell shot out of us, with a thousand yards to go. I peered over the side of the amphtrack and saw another amphtrack three hundred yards to the left get a direct hit from what looked like a mortar shell.

"It's hell in there," said the amphtrack boss, who was pretty wild-eyed himself. "They've already knocked out a lot of amph-tracks and there are a lot of wounded men lying on the beach. See that old hulk of a Jap freighter over there? I'll let you out about there, then go back to get some more men. You can wade in from there." I looked. The rusty old ship was about two hundred yards beyond the pier. That meant some seven hundred yards of wading through the fire of machine guns whose bullets already were whistling over our heads.

The fifteen of us—I think it was fifteen—scurried over the side of the amphtrack into the water that was neck-deep. We started wading.

No sooner had we hit the water than the Jap machine guns really opened up on us. There must have been five or six of these machine guns concentrating their fire on us—there was no nearer target in the water at the time—which meant several hundred bullets per man. I don't believe there was one of the fifteen who wouldn't have sold his chances for an additional twenty-five dollars added to his life-insurance policy. It was painfully slow, wading in such deep water. And we had seven hundred yards to walk slowly into that machine-gun fire, looming into larger targets as we rose onto higher ground. I was scared, as I had never been scared before. But my head was clear. I was extremely alert, as though my brain were dictating that I live these last minutes for all they were worth. I recalled that psychologists say fear in battle is a good thing; it stimulates the adrenalin glands and heavily loads the blood supply with oxygen.

I do not know when it was that I realized I wasn't frightened any longer. I suppose it was when I looked around and saw the amphtrack scooting back for more Marines. Perhaps it was when I noticed that bullets were hitting six inches to the left or six inches to the right. I could have sworn that I could have reached out and touched a hundred bullets. I remember chuckling inside and saying aloud, "You bastards, you certainly are lousy. shots." That, as I told Colonel Carlson next day, was what I later described as my hysteria period. Colonel Carlson, who has been shot at in a number of wars, said he understood.

After wading through several centuries and some two hundred yards of shallowing water and deepening machine-gun fire, I looked to the left and saw that we had passed the end of the pier. I didn't know whether any Jap snipers were still under the pier or not, but I knew we couldn't do any worse. I waved to the Marines on my immediate right and shouted, "Let's head for the pier!" Seven of them came. The other seven Marines were far to the right. They followed a naval ensign straight into the beach—there was no Marine officer in our

amphtrack. The ensign said later that he thought three of the
seven had been killed in the water.

The first three of us lay on the rocks panting, waiting for the
other five to join us. They were laboring heavily to make it,
and bullets from the machine guns on the beach were still
splashing around them like raindrops in a water barrel. By this
time we three were safely hidden from the beach by the thick,
upright, coconut-log stanchions of the pier. I watched these five
men and wondered how on heaven or earth they managed to
come so close to death, yet live. Once I thought the last man,
a short Marine, would not get under the pier. Twenty yards
away, he fell and went under. But he was not hit. In a moment
he was up again, struggling through the water, almost exhausted
beyond further movement, but still carrying his heavy roll of
telephone wire. When he had gone under I had asked myself
whether I had the breath or the courage to go after him. I was
relieved when the necessity of answering the question was obvi-
ated by his arrival.

We were still four hundred yards from the beach. But now
we could crawl in most of the way under the protection of the
pier, where we made difficult, if not altogether invisible, targets. After a few minutes of breath-catching we started crawl-
ing. A hundred yards from the beach, the pier rested on big
coral rocks on the ground, so we had to take to the water again.
It was only a little more than knee-deep now.

I looked on both sides of the pier. Our battalion had been
supposed to land on the right side, but there was no sign of
life anywhere on the right. But on the left there seemed to be
three or four hundred people milling around the beach and
they were wearing, not Jap uniforms, but the spotted brown-
and-green jungle dungarees of the United States Marines. The
eight of us decided to go to the left.

We ducked low, creeping along the edge of the pier. We were
not even shot at. We came upon a stalled bulldozer. This, I reflected, was the American way to fight a war—to try to get a bull-

dozer ashore, even before many men had preceded it. Later I learned that a bulldozer is a fine weapon; it can shovel up sand over a low slit in a pillbox, causing the enemy inside to smother. Two Marines tinkered with the bulldozer, but it had sunk too deep in the water that covered an unseen shellhole. A third Marine lay behind the bulldozer seat. He already had a bullet through his thigh. Then the Jap machine gun chattered, rattling its fire against the frontal blade of the bulldozer. We ducked low behind the machine.

"How goes it?" I asked the Marines.

"Pretty tough," one of them said, matter-of-factly. "It's hell if you climb over that seawall. Those bastards have got a lot of machine guns and snipers back there."

After a few minutes the Jap gave up trying to shoot at the four of us behind the bulldozer. I dashed back to the pier, which was only fifteen feet to the left. During the dash I stepped into a shellhole seven feet deep. Then I swam the rest of the way to the pier.

With each movement of the surf a thousand fish washed against the pier—fish six inches to three feet long. Regardless of their effectiveness against Jap emplacements, shellfire and bombing misses could kill a lot of fish by concussion.

I passed a stalled medium tank, which had floundered when it sank into one of the shellholes. A hundred yards farther to the left there was a stalled light tank. To my surprise I saw a nearly naked figure appear from under the water, swim the last few feet to this tank, then jump in through the top of it. At first I thought it was a Marine who had gone to repair the tank. But why would he take all his clothes off, and why swim under water? Perhaps it was a Jap, but why? I reported the incident when I got ashore, but the officer, with his hands already full, paid little attention to the report. We were to hear later from this stalled tank and from many another disabled tank and amphtrack and boat.

Upon reaching the end of the pier I ducked into a foxhole in the sand which was already crowded with three Marines. I took my first close look at bird-shaped Betio. At this point on the bird's belly, behind the pier that stuck out like a leg, there was a gap. This gap was heaped three or four feet high with sand, but the rest of the island's north rim seemed to be a four-foot seawall built of coconut logs which had been driven into the ground. From the water's edge to the seawall there was twenty feet of sand and brown and green coral. These twenty feet were our beachhead. The Japs controlled the rest of the island, excepting this pocket—twenty feet deep and perhaps a hundred yards wide—which had been established by the Second Battalion of the Eighth Marine Regiment, the farthest left of our three assault battalions, plus two other pockets which had been established as fragilely by the other two battalions. The beginning at Betio did not look bright. But several hundred Marines had gone over that seawall to try to kill the Japs who were killing our men as they waded ashore. They went over—though they knew very well that their chances of becoming a casualty within an hour were something like fifty percent.

I stooped low and ran the hundred feet from the end of the pier to a stalled amphtrack which was jammed against the seawall. Beside the amphtrack a dead Marine lay on the sand. He was the first of many dead Americans I saw on Betio. There was a wide streak of blood on the amphtrack, indicating that the dying man had bled a lot.

A big, red-mustached Marine walked over. "Who is he?" he asked.

"An assistant amphtrack driver, sir," another Marine said. "Name was Cowart. He was twenty years old. He married a girl in Wellington."

"Well, cover him up. Will the amphtrack run?"

"No, sir. We've tried to start it, but I guess the starter was knocked out when this man was killed."

I walked over and introduced myself to the red-mustached Marine. His name was Henry Pierson ("Jim") Crowe and he had been an old-time enlisted man. Now he was a major, commanding the assault battalion that had landed at this point.

"Have you seen any other war correspondents, Major?" I asked. The major said he had not. Poor Frank Filan and Dick Johnston, I thought. They were the A.P. photographer and U.P. reporter who were supposed to land with Crowe's battalion.

The major had other business. Many of his Marines had already gone over the seawall to kill Japs. Now telephone wires were being strung between their forward shellhole posts and his command post behind the stalled amphtrack. I saw a chaplain nearby. I asked him if many men from his battalion had been killed. "I just got here," he said. "I haven't seen but two dead except this man by the amphtrack."

I sat down and leaned against the amphtrack, next to the seawall. Now and then bullets would rattle against the amphtrack, but the seawall made a fairly safe place to sit. With several Marines who were there, wiremen, corpsmen, and battalion staff headquarters men, I felt quite luxurious. If I stayed there, in the dip under the wall, I would be quite safe from any of the Japanese bullets which sang overhead in their high soprano. The Jap mortars, like their guns, were being concentrated on our boats as they approached the shore.

Six hundred yards out, near the end of the pier, I watched a Jap shell hit directly on an LCV that was bringing many Marines ashore. The explosion was terrific and parts of the boat flew in all directions. Then there were many Marines swimming in the water.

Two pairs of corpsmen brought two more dead men and placed them beside the dead boy who had been married to the girl from Wellington. Even now the men had been ashore less than an hour. Yet already the smell of death under the equator's sun could be detected faintly.

Our destroyers were only a thousand yards or so offshore by now and they had begun firing on the tail end of the island, where there were no Americans. The battleships opened up from the other side of the island. Their shells made a great roaring sound when they smacked the land behind where we were sitting. Then we could hear the whish of the shells through the air, then the report from the muzzles of the guns. It seemed odd. It was as though the shells were giving an answer before the question were asked.

I took out my soaked notebooks and opened them up to dry on the hub of the amphtrack. Then I fished the waterproof envelopes out of my wet dungarees. My fine watch was ruined—there was an accumulation of green scum under the crystal. The cigarette lighter in another envelope was also soaked and ruined and already rusted, but the pack of cigarettes was still dry, and they seemed more valuable at the time than either of the other items.

A young Marine walked in front of us, about fifteen feet from where we were sitting, and about five feet from the water's edge. A rifle cracked loudly from behind us. The Marine flinched, grabbed at his head, then ducked to the sand. I thought he had been hit, but, miraculously, he had escaped. He picked up his helmet. There were two inch-wide holes in the top of it, one on each side. The Jap bullet which tore through his helmet had missed his head, but not by more than an eighth of an inch. The Marine's only wound was a scratch on his face, where the helmet had scraped as it was torn savagely off his head.

"All right, god damn it," shouted Major Crowe, "you walk along out there standing up and you're sure as hell going to get shot. Those bastards have got snipers every ten feet back there."

Not fifteen minutes later, in the same spot, I saw the most gruesome sight I had seen in this war. Another young Marine walked briskly along the beach. He grinned at a pal who was sitting next to me. Again there was a shot. The Marine spun all the way around and fell to the ground, dead. From where he lay, a few feet away, he looked up at us. Because he had been shot squarely through the temple his eyes bulged out wide, as in horrific surprise at what had happened to him, though it was impossible that he could ever have known what hit him.

"Somebody go get the son-of-a-bitch," yelled Major Crowe, "He's right back of us here, just waiting for somebody to pass by." That Jap sniper, we knew from the crack of his rifle, was very close.

A Marine jumped over the seawall and began throwing blocks of fused TNT into a coconut-log pillbox about fifteen feet back of the seawall against which we sat. Two more Marines scaled the seawall, one of them carrying a twin-cylindered tank strapped to his shoulders, the other holding the nozzle of the flamethrower. As another charge of TNT boomed inside the pillbox, causing smoke and dust to billow out, a khaki-clad figure ran out the side entrance. The flame thrower, waiting for him, caught him in its withering stream of intense fire. As soon as it touched him, the Jap flared up like a piece of celluloid. He was dead instantly but the bullets in his cartridge belt exploded for a full sixty seconds after he had been charred almost to nothingness. It was the first Jap I saw killed on Betio—the first of four thousand. *Zing, zing, zing*, the cartridge-belt bullets sang. We all ducked low. Nobody wanted to be killed by a dead Jap.

That incident demonstrated something of the characteristics of the Jap sniper. The Jap who killed the grinning Marine had been waiting all morning in the pillbox, not thirty feet from the beach, for just such a shot. Jap snipers are poor marksmen, compared to Marine Corps experts. But at thirty feet not even a poor marksman can miss twice.

I stayed around Major Crowe's battalion headquarters most of that first afternoon, watching the drama of life and death that was being enacted around me. Men were being killed and wounded every minute. The casualties passed along the beach on stretchers, borne by the Navy medical corpsmen who took high losses themselves—out of one group of twenty-nine corpsmen, I heard later, twenty-six were killed or wounded before the battle had ended. But these corpsmen casually, almost slowly, bore their poncho-covered cargo in streams along the beach. The faces of the dead were covered; those of the wounded were not. Once in a while it was possible to load an amphtrack with these wounded and send them back out to the ships which had hospital facilities. Almost any man will go through greater danger to save a friend's life than he will endure in killing the enemy who is the cause of that danger.

The number of dead lined up beside the stalled headquarters amphtrack grew steadily. But the procession of the wounded seemed many times greater. There went a stretcher with a Marine whose leg had been nearly torn off; another had been hit in the buttocks by a 13-mm. bullet or 20-mm. shell—a man's fist could have been thrust into the jagged hole; another was pale as death from the loss of much blood—his face seemed to be all bones and yellowish-white skin and he was in great pain.

From a bomb crater about forty feet over the seawall a strong voice called out during a lull in the big-gun firing, "Major, send somebody to help me! The son-of-a-bitch got me!" Without waiting for orders two corpsmen crawled over the seawall in the face of machine-gun fire which opened up as they appeared. They returned quickly, half dragging, half carrying a husky Marine who had been shot through the bone above his knee. The wounded man, groaning, was sat beside me. "I think he is in that coconut palm," he said, waving his hand in the direction from which he had come. Then he lay down on the sand and inadvertently groaned some more.

A corpsman bandaged the wounded man's leg and jabbed a morphine syrette into his arm. By this time I had been on the island nearly three hours and my notebooks were dried, if wrinkled. I felt that I should do some reporting. I asked the Marine what his name was. It was a very difficult name, and I know I didn't get it right, even after he had spelled it for me twice, but in my notebook it appears as Pfc. N. Laverntine, Jr.

Another Marine who looked no more than nineteen strolled over the seawall. He sat beside the wounded man, smiled, and said, "Bastard got me in the leg, too. I thought I'd stepped on a god-damn mine. It felt like an electric shock." Then he pulled up his trouser leg, showing a neat bullet hole through the fleshy part of his leg. He—his name was Wilson which I could spell —was very deprecating about his wound, which wasn't even bleeding.

Seventy-five yards down the beach, near the end of the pier where I had first landed, the Marines had set up an 81-mm. mortar which they were firing every minute or so. One of them got up to a kneeling position to adjust his instrument. We saw him tumble over the edge of the hole the mortar was set in. Then his companion jumped up to help him. He fell back into the hole. There evidently was another Jap sniper very close to them. I learned later that the first man had been shot through the back; the second who tried to help him had got a bullet through the heart. The men with the TNT and the flamethrower went after a pillbox only a few feet from where the two Marines had been hit. This time the charge of TNT must have been very powerful, because the explosion was as loud as a 75-mm. gun and smoke and dirt flew fifty feet into the air. The sand around the coconut logs was evidently jarred loose, because the flamethrower was sprayed onto the logs, and, although nothing will burn tough, fibrous coconut logs, the flame must have got inside the pillbox. We could hear dozens of bullets popping inside. Later, four dead, charred Japs were found inside the pillbox.

The two wounded men sitting beside me questioned each passerby. "Did —— get killed?" "Have you seen —— or ——?" "You old dope, I thought you were dead." "How's ——? Anybody seen him?" A new arrival sat down beside us and said, "I got more lead in my tail than ever now—that bastard raised up and grinned and threw his grenade. I got sprinkled, but Joe got him."

The three of them carried on a conversation for the rest of the time I stayed there, about an hour. Between rumblings of five-inch destroyer shells that were exploding within a hundred yards, causing the earth to tremble beneath us, I picked up snatches of their talk. They were not afraid, as men might be expected to be who had been shot. They talked quite calmly about what they had seen and speculated on the fate of their comrades. "I know we've already got over twenty-five percent casualties in my company," one said.

Said the latest arrival, a red-head, "Jones was walking by there right after that other fellow got bumped off. A Jap shot off a piece of his thumb. Jones just laughed and kept going."

"That guy has got plenty of guts."

"That Greenwalt has got plenty, too."

"Where's Peterson?"

"I think he's shot."

"T. C. Martin got a leg blown off."

"Very few people ain't got hit."

I do not know what happened to those three wounded Marines. The plan was to evacuate them back to the ships after dark. I hoped they made it all right. I knew such unperturbable men would be needed for other battles.

By four o'clock the naval gunfire and the planes were really raising hell back of us. The destroyer salvos sounded like thunderclaps: the explosion of the hits right back of us, then the whistling of the shell, then the sound of the rumbling of the guns which reached our ears later. The strafing planes—Grumman Hellcats—were coming over now in great numbers, four, six, and eight at a time. First we could see the two wisps of smoke—a gray-blue wisp from the guns on either wing. Then we could hear the popping of the bullets, which sounded like hot grease in a frying pan. They were tearing into the palm trees and the shellholes scattered inland back of us. Then the dive bombers would appear in the sky above us; two or three at a time would dive screamingly toward the earth and let go their bombs. A moment later we would hear the explosions of the bombs—*ka-whump, ka-whump, ka-whump*. And the earth would shudder and more sand would run into our shoes. Then eight more fighters would appear on a line, roaring in at one or two thousand feet overhead, and the sixteen wisps of smoke would trail behind the eight planes, and the grease-popping sounded like a monumental fish-fry. During all these weird, indescribably great noises a Jap machine gun usually chattered incessantly—*poppoppoppop*—as if to show us that all the noise had affected it not at all.

Before I left Major Crowe I noticed a young lieutenant who came into the headquarters area. He walked around completely nonchalant, giving orders to the men with him, while the Jap snipers fired at him steadily. He did not even wear a helmet. I knew that no officer could afford to let his men know he was afraid, but I thought this was carrying it a little too far, this walking around, getting shot at bareheaded. I noted the lieutenant's name—Aubrey Edmonds—because I did not see how he could possibly survive the battle. Later I checked up and found that he had been wounded the second day—shot, not through the head, but in the back.

My friend Lieutenant Hawkins of the Scout and Sniper platoon appeared. "Get down, Hawk, or you'll get shot," somebody yelled at him. The Hawk, who had come back for more ammunition, snarled, "Aw, those bastards can't shoot. They can't hit anything." Then he and the men with him leapt over the seawall again. "Hawk's platoon has been out there all day," an officer told me. "They have knocked out a hell of a lot of machine guns."

I got up about 4:30 to look for my own battalion. Someone had told me that its headquarters were in a shellhole about two hundred yards to the west, on the other side of the pier. When I left Major Crowe's battalion I figured it was getting along pretty well. Casualties were high, but the Marines were whittling away at a lot of machine guns and snipers. The firing from in back of us seemed much less terrific now than it had been three or four hours earlier, though we had stopped trying to land more troops until nightfall, because the Japs were knocking out too many of our boats in the water. From Crowe's headquarters I could count more than fifty disabled tanks, amphtracks, and boats in the water on both sides of the pier. Major Crowe's battalion had a very tough assignment—the Japs drifted up from the tail of the island to the center all through the battle, we learned later, and the supply seemed inexhaustible —but the assignment was not impossible, it seemed.

I stooped low, trying to get down far enough so that the Japs wouldn't be able to see me over the seawall, and walked briskly back along the beach toward the pier. I felt a little ashamed to stoop down, when most of the Marines by now were disdaining the Japs to the extent of walking upright. But I had been shot at and missed so many times during the day that I felt that I didn't want to tempt my luck. By next day I was walking upright, too. I believe that man can get used to anything after a while, even bullets.

The dash across the forty-foot-wide area at the end of the pier, an area which was openly exposed, was dangerous, and almost everyone who tried it was shot at. But I was curious to know what had happened to my own battalion. So I ran across the forty feet, heard three or four bullets sing by, then dropped behind a big coral rock. There was a deep indentation in the coastline at this point. I could walk around the rim, as some reckless Marines were doing, or I could wade through the waist-deep water of the indentation. I chose to wade. When I had reached the beach again I asked a Marine where Second Battalion headquarters was. He pointed to a shellhole under the seawall about a hundred feet ahead. I ran behind the seawall and dropped into the hole.

There I was greeted by three officers I knew: Lieutenant Colonel Irvine Jordan, an observer from another Marine division; "Swede" Norvik, and Lieutenant Odell, the naval aviation liaison man; and Bill Hipple, the A.P. reporter. On Betio everyone was glad to see anyone he knew, because the chances of not seeing him were so heavy. During the six hours since I had landed, for instance, I had become convinced that I was the only correspondent still alive, and I was very glad to see Bill Hipple.

Colonel Jordan was giving a message to a Marine who wrote it down in his yellow book, tore out a sheet, and handed it to a runner who ran up the beach with it. Then he turned to me, "This is really hell. Colonel Amey was killed; his body is lying out there in the water. I was ordered to take over the battalion."

"Where is Major Rice and his staff? Did they make it?" I asked. Ordinarily Major Rice would have taken over the battalion on Colonel Amey's death.

"Haven't heard a word from them. I'm afraid none of them made it. This is all the staff we've got. Odell here has got a bullet through his shoulder, but he's helping."

Said Bill Hipple, "Colonel Amey was right beside me when he was shot. We were within fifty feet of the shore."

Norvik said, "Doc Welte got it, too. He was in our boat."

There were half a dozen Marines in the shellhole headquarters—runners, corpsmen, and communicators. But dozens of others would gather around us, behind the seawall.

"You men, get on up front," Colonel Jordan would say. "They need you out there." A few of the Marines would pick up their guns and head over the seawall, singly, and in twos and threes, but many of them were reluctant to move. Colonel Jordan turned to me, "They don't know me, you see. They haven't got the confidence men should have in their officers."

The firing over the seawall was even heavier than it had been at Major Crowe's headquarters—not so much heavy gunfire and bombing near here, because our own men were scattered through the coconut trees at this point—but every coconut tree seemed to have a Jap sniper in it.

"I don't think E Company has got ten men left," said Norvik, his blue eyes opened wide. This was an exaggeration, of course, as battlefield reports often become exaggerated, but it indicates the extent of the casualties the Second Battalion believed it was taking.*

There were two wounded men in a small, covered Jap coconut-log emplacement on top of the seawall. One of them was in considerable pain and he had a high fever. The other was not hurt badly. He kept a lookout from the rear opening of the emplacement, in case the Japs tried to overwhelm us. On the rim of the shellhole, on the side nearest the water, there were three or four dead Marines. There had not been time to cover them. The dead and the living were so inextricably mixed that it was sometimes difficult to tell one from another.

"How do you feel, Odell?" said Colonel Jordan. "Don't you want to go back to a ship tonight?" Lieutenant Odell grinned and said, "I'm all right. I'll stick it out here. You need all the help you can get."

It was growing dark. It was easy to see that the attack on Betio had not succeeded as we had hoped it would. Our beachhead at Second Battalion headquarters was, like Major Crowe's, only twenty feet wide. Fifty yards to the westward up the beach, and some fifteen yards inland, Colonel Shoup had set up regimental headquarters behind a big Japanese pillbox—the beachhead at that point amounted to perhaps sixty-five or seventy feet.

"All right, men," shouted Norvik, "dig your foxholes. We'll probably get bombed tonight. I want two men to stay on guard for every one who goes to sleep." To others he said, "I want men in foxholes on top of the seawall and as far inland as you can go. If the Japs rush us tonight we've got to be ready for them." A Jap sniper took a shot at Norvik, the shrill *pi-i-ing* whistling

---

* Actually, E Company's casualties were very high. Five of its six officers were killed: Capt. E. G. Walker, Lebanon, Tenn., Lieutenants Maurice F. Reichel, Blytheville, Ark., Louis B. Beck, Cincinnati, William C. Culp, West Palm Beach, Fla., Donald R. Dahlgren, Rector, Mich.

by his ears. He ducked down and continued ordering the defenses of the battalion—or what was left of it.

As darkness began to settle over Tarawa, we could see more Americans heading for shore through the dimming light. "Couple of companies of reinforcements," said an officer. These men were being unloaded at the end of the pier. They could not yet walk along the pier, but they could crawl beneath it and alongside it. The Japs kept trying to pepper them with machine guns and rifles, but their aim generally was not good. Some men would land at the end of the five-hundred-yard pier, and try to walk down it, but the Japs would increase their fire until the Americans usually had to jump into the water or get hit. Even the artillery which was being brought in, 37-mm. anti-tank guns and 75-mm. pack howitzers, were pushed and pulled through the water—they could have been rolled down the pier in one-tenth the time, if it had been possible.

Bill Hipple and I borrowed a shovel—correspondents rarely carry shovels—walked up the·beach about twenty yards, and began looking for a spot to dig a foxhole. We stopped at a coconut-log pillbox and cautiously mounted the seawall to look in it. Inside were four Japs lying beside their machine gun. They were dead.

We jumped off the seawall, back onto the sand. This seemed as good a place as any to dig a foxhole, even if it were only ten feet from four dead Japs who were already beginning to smell. We dug the foxhole wide enough for the two of us, and deep enough so that we would be below the surface of the ground when the Jap bombers came over. We agreed that one would try to sleep while the other stood watch. I knew I was not going to sleep, though I hadn't slept the night before aboard ship —how long ago that seemed, aboard ship! And Bill knew he wasn't going to sleep. For one thing, the Japs would fire their mortars and rifles all night, if only to keep the Marines awake.

I was quite certain that this was my last night on earth. We had twenty feet along perhaps one-sixteenth of one-half of one side of the island, plus a few men in shellholes on either side of the airstrip. The Japs had nearly all the rest. Although we had landed a lot of troops—perhaps three thousand—by this time, most were crowded into such a small space that we did not have room for foxholes to hold them all. And if the Japs counter-attacked, what could we do except shoot at them from behind our seawall until they finally overwhelmed us?

For the first time since morning, I was really scared—this was worse than wading into the machine-gun fire, because the un-known was going to happen under cover of darkness. I tried to joke about it. "Well, Bill," I said, "it hasn't been such a bad life." "Yeah," he said, "but I'm so damned young to die."

My knees shook. My whole body trembled like jelly. I peered into the darkness over the seawall, seeing nothing, hearing noth-ing except an occasional shot from a Jap sniper's rifle. But, I reasoned, it hasn't been a bad life at that. Suppose I don't live until morning? I have already lived fully and quite satisfac-torily. Why should I be afraid to die? My family will be well provided for, with my own insurance and the insurance my company carries on its war correspondents. It will be tough on my children, growing up without a father, but at least they will have a very capable mother and the satisfaction of knowing that their father died in line of duty. And why should any war cor-respondent assume that he can claim exemption from the death that had already come to Colonel Amey and Doc Welte? If I were not here as a war correspondent I would be here as a Marine, anyway. These people made me sick who were always saying, "Oh, what dangers you war correspondents must go through!" I say: war is dangerous, period. And what right has any American to feel that he should not be in it as fully as any other American? This is, I reflected, the United States' war, not the sailors' war or the Marines' war or the soldiers' war. What the hell?

These thoughts were snapped off like a light when a thousand orange-red flashes lit up the sea a couple of miles out. The sky filled with the outpouring of dozens of ships' guns, red balls of fire followed by deafening roars from over the water. "Look, Bill," I cried, "it's a naval battle! All the guns are firing on the surface of the water!" Of course, it was not a naval battle at all. Some low-flying Jap planes had started for the ships in the harbor, and the ships' anti-aircraft guns had opened up on them. They were frightened away and the firing stopped as suddenly as it had started.

Not long afterward a dozen Jap machine guns started chattering at the men on and off the pier, their pink tracer bullets curving out of the palm trees until they were doused in the water. But—of all things, some of this fire was coming from our own disabled boats in the water, and some of it was not the pink of the Jap tracers, but the orange-red stream of our own guns! Our guns, being turned against our own men. It took some time for this to sink in. Then I realized: the Japs had swum out in the darkness to our disabled boats and amphtracks. There they had manned the machine guns we had left in those boats, and now they were shooting at us. Clever, courageous little bastards! They knew it was suicide, but they knew they might kill some Americans before they themselves were killed.

During the night word was passed down the line: the Japs have broken through to the end of the pier. Now we were cut off, even from Major Crowe's battalion. I had not yet heard any word from the other assault battalion which had landed up on the western tip of Betio.

About an hour before dawn we heard the unmistakable purring of a Jap flying-boat's engines. "Old Washing Machine Charley," commented one of the Marines in a nearby foxhole. "I haven't seen him since we were at Guadalcanal. He doesn't do much harm but he keeps you awake." The bomber circled back and forth across the island, evidently trying to find out what was going on down there. Jap machine guns began chattering back of us and pink streams poured toward the beach; the Nips apparently were trying to direct Washing Machine

Charley to us with their effeminate-looking tracers. Charley dropped a couple of bombs, then he flew around a few minutes longer and dropped the rest. They all fell harmlessly into the water. Then he flew away.

During the night I did not see a single Marine fire his rifle. Such firing might have given away our positions. Whatever else, I decided, these Marines were not trigger-happy. They were not forever firing at some figment of their imagination.

THE SECOND DAY

THIS IS HOW THINGS STOOD at dawn of the second day: the three assault battalions held their precarious footholds—Major Crowe's was about midway of the island's north beach, just east of the pier; Lieutenant Colonel Jordan's held a portion of the beach a couple of hundred yards west of Crowe, on the other side of the pier; and the third assault battalion, I learned, had landed on the strongly fortified western tip of the island, on the beak of the Betio bird. This last-named battalion, although separated from its staff and part of its troops, actually had been more successful than the first two. Under the leadership of one of its company commanders, Major Mike Ryan, who took over when the battalion c.o. landed in another pocket, it had fought its way inland until it held a seventy-yard beachhead before dark of the first day. The naval gunfire had been particularly effective on this western end of the island, knocking out all the big guns which had been the chief defense, and Major Ryan's men had, in the words of Colonel Shoup, proved themselves "a bunch of fighting fools." The battalion, of course, was isolated from the rest of the Marines on the island.

During the first night the Japs, apparently because their communications had been disrupted and many of their men undoubtedly had been stunned, had not counterattacked. Probably as many as three hundred Japs, we learned later, had committed suicide under the fierce pounding of our naval guns and bombs.

Meanwhile, the Marines had landed Colonel Shoup's combat team reserve battalion, the first battalion of the Second Regiment. During the night considerable quantities of ammunition, some artillery, some tanks (light and medium), and other supplies had also been brought in.

General Julian Smith had sent a message from his battleship headquarters: "Attack at dawn; division reserve will start landing at 0600." The division reserve was the first and third battalions of the Eighth Marines.

Our casualties had been heavy on the first day, but well over half the dead, and practically all of the wounded, had been shot, not in the water, but after they had reached land and climbed the seawall. Those wounded more than lightly in the water had little chance of reaching shore. The amphibious operation up to that point, therefore, could have been called better than successful. The hell lay in the unexpectedly strong fortifications we had found after we landed.

It was not possible—and never will be possible—to know just how many casualties the three assault battalions had suffered D Day. Most officers agreed afterward that thirty-five to forty percent was as good a guess as any. Effectively, they were groggy if they had not been knocked out, because their organization was ripped to pieces. Their percentage casualties among officers had been heavier than among the men, and key men such as platoon sergeants, virtually irreplaceable, had been killed or wounded. Therefore, we had to have more men quickly, and General Smith had said they were on the way.

Because the second day was even more critical than the first, and because it was the day the tide finally turned in our favor, I have written a play-by-play chronology (as I saw it) from my notes:

0530: The coral flats in front of us present a sad sight at low tide. A half dozen Marines lie exposed, now that the water has receded. They are hunched over, rifles in hand, just as they fell. They are already one-quarter covered by sand that the high tide left. Further out on the flats and to the left I can see at least fifty other bodies. I had thought yesterday, however, that low tide would reveal many more than that. The smell of death, that sweetly sick odor of decaying human flesh, is already oppressive.

Now that it is light, the wounded go walking by, on the beach. Some are supported by corpsmen; others, like this one coming now, walk alone, limping badly, their faces contorted with pain. Some have bloodless faces, some bloody faces, others only pieces of faces. Two corpsmen pass, carrying a Marine on a stretcher who is lying face down. He has a great hole in his side, another smaller hole in his shoulder. This scene, set against the background of the dead on the coral flats, is horrible. It is war. I wish it could be seen by the silken-voiced, radio-announcing pollyannas back home who, by their very inflections, nightly lull the people into a false sense of all-is-well.

0600: One of the fresh battalions is coming in. Its Higgins boats are being hit before they pass the old hulk of a freighter seven hundred yards from shore. One boat blows up, then another. The survivors start swimming for shore, but machine-gun bullets dot the water all around them. Back of us the Marines have started an offensive to clean out the Jap machine guns which are now firing at our men in the water. They evidently do not have much success, because there is no diminution of the fire that rips into the two dozen or more Higgins boats. The *ratatatatatat* of the machine guns increases, and the high *pi-i-ing* of the Jap sniper bullet sings overhead incessantly. The Japs still have some mortars, too, and at least one 40- or 77-mm. gun. Our destroyers begin booming their five-inch shells on the Jap positions near the end of the airfield back of us.

Some of the fresh troops get within two hundred yards of shore, while others from later waves are unloading further out. One man falls, writhing in the water. He is the first man I have seen actually hit, though many thousands of bullets cut into the water. Now some reach the shore, maybe only a dozen at first. They are calm, even disdainful of death. Having come this far, slowly, through the water, they show no disposition to hurry. They collect in pairs and walk up the beach, with snipers still shooting at them. ·

Now one of our mortars discovers one of the machine guns that has been shooting at the Marines. It is not back of us, but is a couple of hundred yards west, out in one of the wooden privies the dysentery-fearing Japs built out over the water. The mortar gets the range, smashes the privy, and there is no more firing from there.

But the machine guns continue to tear into the oncoming Marines. Within five minutes I see six men killed. But the others keep coming. One rifleman walks slowly ashore, his left arm a bloody mess from the shoulder down. The casualties become heavier. Within a few minutes more I can count at least a hundred Marines lying on the flats.

0730: The Marines continue unloading from the Higgins boats, but fewer of them are making the shore now. Many lie down behind the pyramidal concrete barriers the Japs had erected to stop tanks. Others make it as far as the disabled tanks and amphtracks, then lie behind them to size up the chances of making the last hundred yards to shore. There are at least two hundred bodies which do not move at all on the dry flats, or in the shallow water partially covering them. This is worse, far worse than it was yesterday.

Now four of our carrier-based fighters appear over the water. The first makes a glide and strafes the rusty freighter hulk, then the second, third, and fourth. Thousands of their fifty-caliber bullets tear into the old ship, each plane leaving a dotted, blue-gray line behind each wing. "The god-damn Japs must have swum out there last night and mounted a machine gun in that freighter," says an officer beside me. "I thought I saw some bullets coming this way."

Three more Hellcats appear. These carry small bombs under their bellies. The first dives for the freighter and misses by at least fifty yards. The second does likewise. But the third gets a direct hit and the old freighter gushes a flame fifty feet into the air. But the flame apparently is from the bomb explosion alone, because it dies out immediately. "May kill some of our own men out there with that bombing and strafing," observes the officer, "but we've got to do it. That Jap machine gun is killing our men in the water." A dozen more bomber-fighters appear in the sky. One after another they glide gracefully to within a few hundred feet of the freighter, drop their bombs, and sail away. But only one of the twelve gets a hit on the freighter. I am surprised at their inaccuracy—one bomb is two hundred yards beyond the target. These fighter-bombers are less accurate than the more experienced dive bombers.

0800: Back at Colonel Jordan's command post nobody is happy. Things are still going badly. Colonel Jordan is talking to Major Crowe: "Are there many snipers behind your front lines? Uh, huh, we have a hell of a lot, too."

"Where is my little runner? Where is Paredes?" asks Colonel Jordan.

"He is dead, Colonel. He was killed right over there," a Marine answers. Corporal Osbaldo R. Paredes of Los Angeles was a brave Marine. All during the first day he had carried messages through intense fire, never hesitating to accept the most dangerous mission. "Oh, hell!" says the misty-eyed colonel. "What a fine boy! I'll certainly see that his family gets the Navy Cross." He stops suddenly. The Navy Cross seems quite inadequate now, only a few minutes after Paredes has been killed.

By now all the coconut trees from which snipers had been shot yesterday are filled again with more snipers. The sniper fire seems more frequent than ever and nobody can stick his head out of the battalion shellhole without getting shot at. The hell of it is that they are in trees only a few yards away, and they are hard to spot. They are not dangerous at any respectable range, but from their nearby positions they can kill a lot of Marines. A Marine comes by headquarters grinning. "I just got one," he says. "He dropped his rifle on the third shot, and it fell at my feet. But I swear I haven't seen him yet. I guess they tie themselves to trees just like they did at Guadalcanal."

0830: By now most of the Marines have arrived who will ever get ashore from those waves that were hit so badly early this morning. Those lying behind the tank blocks and the disabled boats get up once in a while and dash for shore. But I'm afraid we lost two hundred of them this morning, maybe more.

A captain comes by and reports that one of his men has singl-handedly knocked out eight machine-gun nests—five yesterday and three this morning. Another unattached officer, whose normal duty is a desk job, not combat, drops in and reports that he finally killed a sniper. He had been out looking all morning— "How can you kill the bastards if you can't see them?"—and he finally had fired a burst into a coconut palm. Out dropped a Jap, wearing a coconut-husk cap. We feel that we are eliminating a lot of Jap machine gunners and snipers now. As the last men come ashore, there is only one machine gun firing at them, and it hits nobody.

0940: Now the high explosives are really being poured on the Jap positions toward the tail end of the island. Our 75-mm. pack howitzers are firing several rounds a minute. The strafing planes are coming over by the dozens, and the dive bombers by the half-dozens. Now we have many 81-mm. mortars joining the deathly orchestra. Betio trembles like a leaf, but I ask myself, "Are we knocking out many of those pillboxes?"

We know the Japs are still killing and wounding a lot of men. The stretchers are passing along the beach again, carrying their jungle-cloth-covered burdens. One Marine on a stretcher is bandaged around the head, both arms, and both legs. One of the walking wounded, his left arm in a white sling, walks slowly along the beach in utter contempt of the sniper who fires at him. *1100:* Finally at Colonel Shoup's headquarters. And what a headquarters! Fifteen yards inland from the beach, it is a hole dug in the sand back of a huge pillbox that probably was some kind of Japanese headquarters. The pillbox is forty feet long, eight feet wide, and ten feet high. It is constructed of heavy coconut logs, six and eight inches in diameter. The walls of the pillbox are two tiers of coconut logs, about three feet apart. The logs are joined together by eight-inch steel spikes, shaped like a block letter C. In between the two tiers of logs are three feet of sand, and covering the whole pillbox several more feet of sand are heaped. No wonder our bombs and shells hadn't destroyed these pillboxes! Two-thousand-pound bombs hitting directly on them might have partially destroyed them, but bombing is not that accurate--not even dive bombing—on as many pillboxes as the Japs have on Betio. And when bombs hit beside such structures they only throw up more sand on top of them.

Colonel Shoup is nervous. The telephone shakes in his hand. "We are in a mighty tight spot," he is saying. Then he lays down the phone and turns to me, "Division has just asked me whether we've got enough troops to do the job. I told them no. They are sending the Sixth Marines, who will start landing right away." Says a nearby officer: "That damned Sixth is cocky enough already. Now they'll come in and claim they won the battle." *

From his battalion commanders Colonel Shoup receives regular telephone reports. One of them is now asking for air

* The Sixth is one of the two Marine regiments which fought so bravely and brilliantly in France in World War I. But other regiments are jealous of the Sixth's honors. Examples: (1) in Shanghai it used to be said that the "pogey-bait" Sixth ordered $40,000 worth of post-exchange supplies—one dollar's worth of soap, the rest in candy ("pogey-bait"); (2) in New Zealand other Marines spread the rumor that the *fourragère* which the Sixth's men wore on their shoulders indicated that the wearer had a venereal disease.

bombardment on a Jap strongpoint on the other side of the airfield, which we can see a few hundred feet from regimental headquarters. "All right," says the colonel, putting down the telephone. "Air liaison officer!" he calls, "tell them to drop some bombs on the southwest edge of 229 and the southeast edge of 231. There's some Japs in there giving us hell." The numbers refer to the keyed blocks on the map of the island. It seems less than ten minutes before four dive bombers appear overhead, then scream toward the earth with their bombs, which explode gruffly: *ka-whump, ka-whump, ka-whump, ka-whump.* Even nearer than the bombs, destroyer shells in salvos of four are bursting within ten minutes after a naval liaison officer has sent directions by radio.

Next to regimental quarters rises a big, uncompleted barracks building, which withstood our bombing and shelling very well. There are only a few small holes in the roof and wooden sides of the building. Five-foot tiers of coconut logs surround the building, to protect it against shrapnel. I run the thirty feet from Colonel Shoup's command post eastward to the tier and leap over it. Some Marines are in the unfloored building, lying on the ground, returning a Jap sniper's fire which comes from we know not where. Says a Marine: "That god-damn smokeless powder they've got beats anything we ever had." Then I cross the interior of the building, go through a hole in the wall and sit down beside some Marines who are in the alleyway between the wooden building and the tier of coconut logs.

"This gets monotonous," says a Marine as a bullet whistles through the alley. We are comparatively safe, sitting here, because we are leaning against the inside of the log tier, and the vertical logs that act as braces are big enough for us to squeeze behind. The problem is to flatten one's legs against the ground so that they are not exposed to the sniper's fire.

1130: These Marines are from H Company, the heavy-weapons company of the battalion I came with. "We've already had fifteen men killed, more in twenty-four hours than we had on

Guadalcanal in six months," said the Marine sitting next to me, "and I don't know how many wounded."

"We started in in one amphib, and it got so hot the driver drove off before he had unloaded all of us. Then the amphib sank—it had been hit—and another one picked us up and brought us ashore."

Where had they landed? "Right over there by that pillbox with the four Japs in it," he replies, pointing to the spot near which Bill Hipple and I had dug our foxhole. "You know who killed those Japs? Lieutenant Doyle of G Company did it—that's P. J. Doyle from Neola, Iowa—he just tossed a grenade in, then he jumped in with the Japs and shot them all with his carbine before they could shoot him."

By now it is fairly raining sniper bullets through our alley, as if the sniper is desperate because he isn't hitting anybody. The sniper is evidently a couple of hundred yards away, because there is a clear space that is far back from the open end of the alley. Japs can hide behind a coconut log without being seen all day, but nobody ever heard of one hiding behind a grain of sand.

A bullet ricochets off the side of the barracks building and hits the leg of the private who is second down the line. "I'm glad that one was spent," he says, picking up the .303-caliber copper bullet, which is bent near the end of the nose. I reach out for the bullet and he hands it to me. I drop it quickly because it is almost as hot as a live coal. The Marines all laugh.

These Marines calmly accept being shot at. They've grown used to it by now, and I suddenly realize that it is to me no longer the novelty it was. It seems quite comfortable here, just bulling. But I am careful to stay behind the upright coconut log which is my protection against the sniper.

Into the alleyway walks a Marine who doesn't bother to seek the protection of the coconut logs. He is the dirtiest man I have seen on the island—men get dirty very quickly in battle, but this one has a good quarter inch of gray-black dust on his beardless face and his dungarees are caked. A lock of blond hair sticks out from under his helmet.

"Somebody gimme some cigarettes," he says. "That machine-gun crew is out there in a shell-hole across the airfield and there's not a cigarette in the crowd." One of the Marines throws him a pack of Camels.

The new arrival grins. "I just got me another sniper. That's six today, and me a cripple." I ask if he has been shot. "Hell, no," he says, "I busted my ankle stepping into a shellhole yesterday." His name? "Pfc. Adrian Strange." His home? "Knox City, Texas." Age? "Twenty."

Pfc. Adrian Strange stands for a few minutes, fully exposed to the sniper who has been pecking at us. Then the sniper opens up again, the bullets rattling against the coconut logs.

Pfc. Strange sings out, "Shoot me down, you son-of-a-bitch." Then he leisurely turns around and walks back across the airfield, carrying his carbine and the pack of cigarettes.

"That boy Strange," says the Marine next to me, "he just don't give a damn."

1200: Colonel Shoup has good news. Major Ryan's short-handed battalion has crossed the western end of the island (the bird's head), and the entire eight-hundred-yard beach up there is now ours. There are plenty of Japs just inside the beach, and the fortifications on the third of the island between Shoup's command post and Ryan's beach are very strong. And the entire south shore of the island, where there are even stronger pillboxes than there were on the north, remains to be cleaned out. That is the job of the Sixth Regiment, which will land this afternoon.

A young major comes up to the colonel in tears. "Colonel, my men can't advance. They are being held up by a machine gun." Shoup spits, "Goddlemighty, one machine gun."

1215: Here the Marines have been sitting in back of this pill-box (Shoup's headquarters) for twenty-four hours. And a Jap just reached out from an air vent near the top and shot Corporal

Oliver in the leg. In other words, there have been Japs within three feet—the thickness of the wall—of the Marines' island commander all that time. Three Japs had been killed in the pillbox yesterday, and we thought that was all there were.

There is very bad news about Lieutenant Hawkins. He may die from his three wounds. He didn't pay much attention to the shrapnel wound he got yesterday, but he has been shot twice this morning. He wouldn't be evacuated when he got a bullet through one shoulder. "I came here to kill Japs; I didn't come here to be evacuated," he said. But a while ago he got a bullet through the other shoulder, and lower down. He lost a lot of blood from both wounds.

Said the corporal who told me this, "I think the Scout and Sniper platoon has got more guts than anybody else on the island. We were out front and Morgan (Sergeant Francis P. Morgan of Salem, Oregon) was shot in the throat. He was bleeding like hell, and saying in a low voice, 'Help me, help me.' I had to turn my head."

Lieutenant Paine, who had been nicked in the rear as he stood talking to us—"I'll be damned. I stay out front four hours, then I come back to the command post and get shot"—has more news about Hawkins. "He is a madman," says Paine. "He cleaned out six machine-gun nests, with two to six Japs in each nest. I'll never forget the picture of him standing on that amph-track, riding around with a million bullets a minute whistling by his ears, just shooting Japs. I never saw such a man in my life."

The young major whose men were held up by a single machine gun was back again. "Colonel, there are a thousand god-damn Marines out there on that beach, and not one will follow me across to the air strip," he cries, desperately. Colonel Jordan, who by this time was back at his old job as observer, our battalion having been merged with Major Wood Kyle's reinforcing first battalion, speaks up, "I had the same trouble. Most of them are brave men, but some are yellow." I recall something a very wise general once told me, "In any battle you'll find the fighting men up front. Then you'll find others who will linger behind, or find some excuse to come back. It has always been that way, and it always will. The hell of it is that in any battle you lose a high percentage of your best men."

Says Colonel Shoup, "You've got to say, 'Who'll follow me?' And if only ten follow you, that's the best you can do, but it's better than nothing."

1300: Now they are bringing up the dead for burial near the command post. There are seven laid out about ten yards from where I sit. They are covered with green and brown ponchos, only their feet sticking out. I think: what big feet most American soldiers and Marines have! None of those looks smaller than a size eleven. The stench of the dead, as the burial detail brings them past and lines them up on the ground, is very heavy now.

Somebody brings in the story of a Jap sniper whose palm-tree roost was sprayed repeatedly. But he kept on firing, somehow. Finally, in disgust, a sergeant took a machine gun and fired it until he had cut the tree in two, near the top. The fall is supposed to have killed the Jap.

1430: Things look better now. The amphtracks—those that are left—are bringing stuff ashore and carrying the wounded regularly, and they get shot at only occasionally when they head back into the water. Major Ryan and his crowd are doing very well at the western end of the island, and the Sixth Marines are about to land there and start down the south shore. We've got another company of light tanks ashore, and they are going up as close as possible to the Jap pillboxes and firing high explosives into the slits. The improved situation is reflected in everyone's face around headquarters.

1600: Bill Hipple and I head east along the beach to Major Crowe's headquarters. By this time we are so confident that the battle is running in our favor that we do not even crouch down, as we walk four feet apart, one ahead of another. After we cross the base of the pier the inevitable sniper's bullet sings by. "Jesus," says Hipple, "do you know that damned bullet went between us?" We crouch down under the protection of the seawall during the rest of the journey.

That tough, old-time Marine, Jim Crowe, is having a tough time yet, but he is still as cool as icebox lettuce. "We kill 'em and more come filtering up from the tail of the island," he says. I ask him about his casualties. "Already had about three hundred in my battalion," he says.

A young tank officer, Lieutenant L. E. Larbey, reports to the major as we are talking to him. "I just killed a Marine, Major Crowe," he says bitterly. "Fragments from my 75 splintered against a tree and ricocheted off. God damn, I hated for that to happen."

"Too bad," mutters Crowe, "but it sometimes happens. Fortunes of war."

The heavy tanks are being used against the pillboxes. They have tried crushing them, but even a thirty-two-ton tank is not very effective against these fortifications. "We got a prisoner last night," said Crowe, "and we have four more, temporarily, sealed up in a pillbox. I suppose they'll kill themselves before we get 'em out."

The strafing planes are coming overhead in waves now and the grease-popping sound of their guns is long and steady. "Don't know how much good they do," says Crowe, "but we know their bullets will kill men if they hit anything. One fifty-caliber slug hit one of my men—went through his shoulder, on down through his lung and liver. He lived about four minutes. Well, anyway, if a Jap ever sticks his head out of his pillbox the planes may kill him."

1630: Crowe is talking on the phone, apparently to Colonel Shoup: "I suggest we hold a line across from the Burns-Philp pier tonight." That means his men have advanced about two hundred yards to the east, toward the tail of the island, and he believes they can hold a line all the way across the island, which is about six hundred yards wide at that point. Meantime, my old battalion, plus the reinforcements, are cleaning out the center of the island, Major Ryan's battalion is holding the western end, and a battalion of the Sixth Marines is landing to start down the southern shore (the Betio bird's back). We can see the light now. We are winning, but we've still got to dig out every last Jap from every last pillbox, and that will cost us a lot of Marines. I reflect: isn't that true of our whole war against the Japs? They haven't got a chance and they know it, unless we get fainthearted and agree to some kind of peace with them. But, in an effort to make us grow sick of our losses, they will hang on under their fortifications, like so many bedbugs. They don't care how many men *they* lose—human life being a minor consideration to them. The Japs' only chance is our getting soft, as they predicated their whole war on our being too luxury-loving to fight.

Of this much I am certain: the Marines are not too soft to fight. More than three thousand of them are by this time assaulting pillboxes full of the loathsome bugs, digging them out.

1700: Hipple and I are surprised to see two more correspondents—we had long since decided that none others were alive. But Dick Johnston, a young, pencil-thin U.P. man, and Frank ("Fearless") Filan, A.P. photographer, had also managed to land with the assault waves. "Filan, here," says Johnston, "is a hero. The Marine next to him was shot as they waded in. Filan started helping him back to the boat. But then a sniper opened up on the boat from the side. The Marine beat Filan to the shore. And Filan ruined all his cameras and equipment helping the Marine." The two correspondents report that at least one more correspondent arrived this morning. Don Senick, the newsreelman. "His boat was turned back yesterday," says Johnston, "but they got ashore this morning. Senick ought to get the Purple Heart. He was sitting under a coconut tree. A bullet hit above his head and dropped on his leg. It bruised him."

Lieutenant Larbey sits down beside us. "Were you ever inside a tank when it got hit?" he asks. "The spot inside the tank where the shell hits turns a bright yellow, like a sunrise. My tank got two hits a while ago." Larbey walks back to his iron horse. Says Johnston, "That guy is a genius at keeping his tanks running. He repairs the guns, refuels them somehow, and reloads them with ammunition."

A tall, grinning Marine is here at headquarters getting ammunition. He has a bandage on his arm, and a casualty tag around his neck like those the corpsmen put on every man they treat—in case he collapses later from his wound.

"Get shot in the arm?" asks Jim Crowe.

"Yes, sir," says Morgan.

"What'd you do, stick your arm out of a foxhole, eh?"

"No, sir, I was walking alongside a tank." And Morgan goes on about his business, gathering ammunition. Crowe looks up at the sky, which is full of planes. "Look at them god-damn strafing planes. They haven't killed fifty Japs in two days," he growls.

A grimy Marine seated alongside us muses: "I wonder what our transport did with those sixteen hundred half pints of ice cream that was to be sent ashore yesterday after the battle was over."

An officer comes in and reports to Major Crowe that a sniper is raising hell with the people working on supplies at the end of the pier. By this time we are stacking great piles of supplies on the end of the pier. The officer thinks the fire is coming, not from the beach, but from a light tank that is half sunk in the water. It is the same tank that I saw the naked figure dive into as I came ashore. These devilish Japs!

A destroyer standing so close to shore that it must be scraping bottom has been ordered to fire at a big concrete blockhouse a couple of hundred yards away from us. First, it fires single rounds—five or six of them. Then, when the range is found, it opens up with four guns at a time and to us it seems that all bedlam has broken loose. After about eighty rounds it stops.

"They never hit it squarely," says Major Crowe, "but almost."

1803: Now, at three minutes past six, the first two American jeeps roll down the pier, towing 37-mm. guns. "If a sign of certain victory were needed," I note, "this is it. The jeeps have arrived."

1900: Back at regimental headquarters, Colonel Shoup wipes his red forehead with his grimy sleeve and says, "Well, I think we are winning, but the bastards have got a lot of bullets left." I ask him how much longer it would last. "I believe we'll clean up the entire western end of the island tomorrow, maybe more. It will take a day or two more to root them all out of the tail end of the island."

A surgeon grunts and rises from where he has been working feverishly over a dozen wounded Marines who lie on the beach. His blood-plasma containers hang from a line strung between a pole and a bayoneted rifle stuck upright into the ground. Four deathly pale Marines are receiving the plasma through tubes in their arms. "These four will be all right," the doctor thinks, "but there are a lot more up the beach that we probably can't save." He continues, "This battle has been hell on the medical profession. I've got only three doctors out of the whole regiment. The rest are casualties, or they have been lost or isolated. By now nearly all the corpsmen have been shot, it seems to me."

Lieutenant Colonel Presley M. Rixey, a blue-eyed, mustachioed Virginian who commands the artillery attached to Colonel Shoup's regimental combat team, is the first man I have heard pick the turning point of the battle, "I thought up until one o'clock today it was touch and go. Then I knew we would win. It's not over yet, but we've got 'em." Supplies are beginning to flow over the pier in quantity now. The last of Colonel Rixey's 37's and 75's are being landed, "at long last," he says.

"You know what," says Colonel Rixey, "I'll bet these are the heaviest casualties in Marine Corps history. I believe we've already lost more than ten percent of the division and we haven't

landed all of it." Until now I haven't considered Tarawa in the
light of history. It has only seemed like a brawl—which it is—
that we might easily have lost, but for the superb courage of the
Marines. But, I conclude, Colonel Rixey may have something
there. Maybe this is history.*

1930: Hipple and I begin digging our foxhole for the night—
this time a hundred yards further up the beach, next to Amphtrack No. 10. "This one came in on the first wave," says a
nearby Marine, "there were twenty men in it, and all but three
of them were killed."

As we dig deeper, the smell from our foxhole becomes oppressive. "Not all the Japs used those privies over the water,"
I commented. Hipple has finished digging with the shovel, and
now he begins smoothing the foxhole with his hands—all foxholes should be finished by hand. The smell is so oppressive we
throw a few shovelfuls of sand back into the hole to cover at
least some of the odor.

Then we lie down to sleep. It has been more than sixty hours
since we closed our eyes and the danger of a night attack has
been all but eliminated, so we sleep soundly.

2400: We are rudely awakened after three hours' sleep. The
tide has come up and flooded our foxhole. This is unusual, because the tide has not been this high since we reached the
island. We sit on a bank of sand, wide-awake and knowing that
there will be no more sleep tonight. Besides, Washing Machine
Charley will be due soon and nobody can sleep while being
bombed.

0500: Washing Machine Charley was over at four o'clock. He
dropped eight bombs in his two runs over the island. Said Keith
Wheeler, later, "He was absolutely impartial; he dropped half
his bombs on us and half on the Japs." Water or no water, we
lay face down in our foxhole as he came over. As the bombs

At Soissons July 19, 1918, the Marines suffered 1,303 casualties. They probably took more the first day on Tarawa, and the ratio of dead to wounded was
1 to 2 instead of 1 to 10.

hit, there was a blinding flash a couple of hundred yards up the beach, to the west. A few minutes later a Marine came running up the beach, shouting, "There are a lot of men hurt bad up here. Where are the corpsmen and the stretchers?" He was directed to a pile of stretchers nearby. Soon the stretcher bearers returned, silhouetted by the bright half-moon as they walked along the beach. Washing Machine Charley had killed one man, had wounded seven or eight.

0530: At first light, Bill Hipple looks at what had been our foxhole. Then he learns that the odor was caused, not by Jap excrement, but by the body of a dead man who had been buried beside the foxhole. Bill had been clawing the face of a dead man as he put the finishing touches on the foxhole.

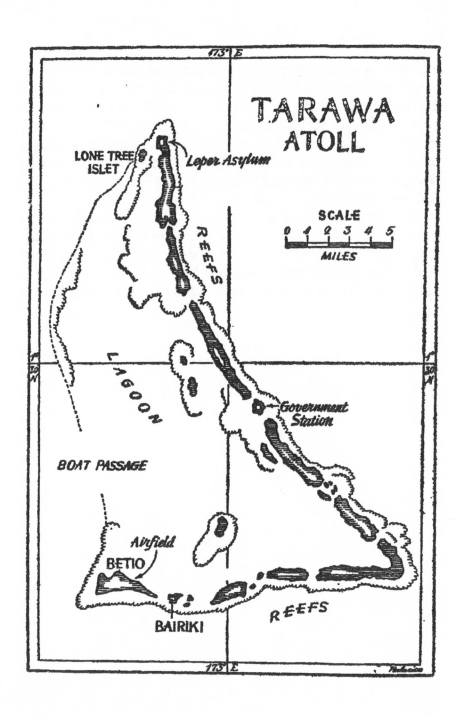

TARAWA
ATOLL

SCALE
0 1 2 3 4 5
MILES

LONE TREE
ISLET

Leper Asylum

R E E F S

L A G O O N

Government
Station

BOAT PASSAGE

Airfield
BETIO

BAIRIKI

R E E F S

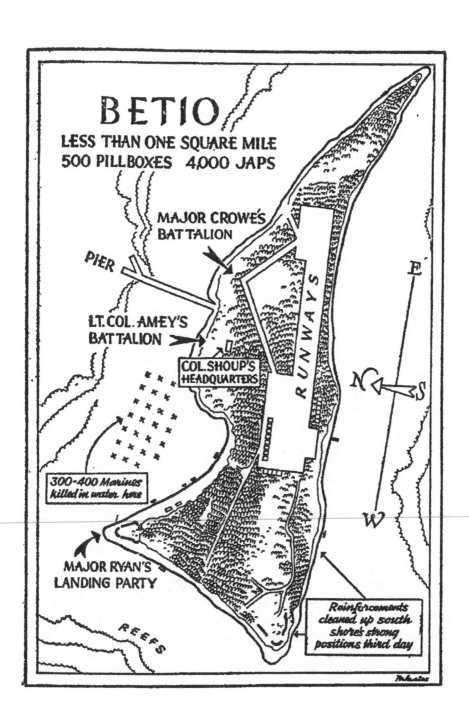

BETIO

LESS THAN ONE SQUARE MILE
500 PILLBOXES   4,000 JAPS

MAJOR CROWE'S
BATTALION

PIER

LT. COL. AMEY'S
BATTALION

COL. SHOUP'S
HEADQUARTERS

RUNWAYS

E

N   S

W

300-400 Marines
killed in water here

MAJOR RYAN'S
LANDING PARTY

REEFS

Reinforcements
cleaned up south
shore's strong
positions third day

THE THIRD DAY

THIS WAS THE DAY the Japs fell apart. There were many factors in this rout. Another company of light tanks and a few thirty-two-ton tanks had a field day with the Japs, who cowered in their pillboxes and waited for death. Armored half-tracks, mounting 75-mm. guns, paraded up and down Betio all day, pouring high explosives into pillboxes, carrying Marine riflemen who killed Japs whenever they dared stick their heads up. The men with the flamethrowers killed many hundreds in their fortifications, or outside their fortifications. Our line across the island had held during the night, preventing any fresh Japs from filtering toward the scenes of the toughest fighting. On the third day the question was not, "How long will it take to kill them all?" but, "How few men can we expect to lose before killing the rest of the Japs?"

But probably the biggest factor on the third day was Major William Jones' first battalion of the Sixth Marines, who jumped off at dawn from their landing point on the southwestern tip of the island and marched straight up the beach that is the Betio bird's back. The Sixth took heavy casualties—the fortifications on this south beach were even stronger than those on the lagoon side of the island—but they swung ahead quickly and violently, like men who were anxious to get it over with. Lieutenant Colonel McLeod's third battalion of the Sixth landed on the western beach in the early morning and marched through Major Ryan's depleted forces, cleaning out huge fortifications as they went along, walking beside medium tanks which bored into the fading Japs.

Commented Lieutenant Colonel Evans Carlson in mid-morning, "These Marines are in the groove today." Lieutenant Colonel Jordan, who had been distressed earlier because some of the Marines hung back on the beaches, was proud of these same men today. "Tell you something interesting. Once we got those men off the beaches and up front, they were good. They waded into the Japs and proved they could fight just as well as anybody."

During the day I saw the first five of many Japs I saw who committed suicide rather than fight to the end. In one hole, under a pile of rubble, supported by a tin roof, four of them had removed the split-toed, rubber-soled jungle shoes from their right feet, had placed the barrels of their .303 rifles against their foreheads, then had pulled the triggers with their big toes. The other had chosen the same method some five hundred Japs chose on Attu: holding a hand grenade against his chest, thus blowing out the chest and blowing off the right hand. From the time he was a baby the Jap had been told that he was superior to the white man, and all he had to do to win was to fight aggressively. When he found that this was not true, and the white man could fight aggressively, too, he became frustrated. He had never been taught to improvise and his reflexes were hopelessly slow; if his plan of battle failed, as the Jap plan on Tarawa failed when the first Marines made the shore, he was likely, under pressure, to commit suicide. He didn't know what else to do.

This is the way I recorded what I saw on Betio the third day:

0600: The destroyers open up on the tail end of the island from very close range. Their targets are immense concrete blockhouses, which they are determined to penetrate if it takes dozens of five-inch rounds in the same precise spot on the wall. It is reported that three hundred Japs are in one of these blockhouses. The 75 howitzers, firing rapidly, are concentrating on the same area and the noise is greater than it has been before. The captain of A Battery is reported dead—shot through the head by a sniper.

Two dead Japs in a crater just behind our last night's foxholes have been discovered wearing Marine helmets, jungle dungarees and boondockers.

A corpsman comes by and sits down to chat. He found a dead Marine under the edge of the pier, in a position where he might not have been discovered for days. From the dead Marine's pack the corpsman had taken two cans of corned beef, two wet packs of Lucky Strikes, a soaked wallet containing a letter and some airmail stamps and an identification card: "William F. Pasco . . . born March, 1923." The corpsman knows he shouldn't have removed a dead man's identification—because of the confusion that might result if the corpsman himself is killed or wounded later, but like so many well-meaning soldiers and Marines—"I thought I'd send the stuff home to his folks."

0630: Now the destroyers have let up momentarily and the dive bombers and strafing fighters are vying with each other to see who can tear up the tail end of the island. This goes on unceasingly for a half hour, with probably more than two hundred planes taking part. The isolated Japs on that end of the island must know that our determination to take Betio has not weakened. By now our own troops are dispersed so widely over the island that the bombers concentrate only on the tail-end third. When the planes have finished, the destroyers and artillery open up more furiously than ever. Sometimes the whole island shakes until it seems ready to disappear into the ocean—as the battleship gunnery officers threatened it would. But we doubt that it will.

0700: Here, a hundred yards inland from the beach, is the type of fortification that has withstood this awful pounding for two days, and it is no wonder! Double thicknesses of eight-inch-thick coconut logs, hooked together with steel spikes, buttressed by upright logs driven far into the ground, covered by three feet of shrapnel-absorbing sand. The pillbox cannot be built altogether underground because water lies only four to six feet under the surface on Betio, so it is half underground and half above ground. Dick Johnston, the U.P. correspondent, marvels at the almost impregnable construction when a Marine engineer comes along and says, "You've got to give them credit. They've got a good engineer somewhere in this Jap Navy." At the sunken entrance to the pillbox two Marines are warming a can of C ration on a folding field stove over a Sterno flame. We put a can of the C ration—vegetable and beef hash—over the flame and eat a heavy breakfast of our own. For the first time it occurs to me that I haven't eaten in two days.

Nearby there is a chicken yard containing about twenty chickens, including two dead ones, and a coop inhabited by two small black and white ducks. Although the area is still under sniper fire a boyish Marine chases an escaped chicken, then dives heartily after the bird, but misses. The two Marines eating with us guffaw. Says one, "I almost opened up on a pig last night."

Johnston is tempted to take a flashlight, go into one of the pillboxes to hunt souvenirs. But the smell at the entrance is so oppressive he is easily dissuaded. Some Marines tell us that there are twelve dead Japs inside. An apocryphal story going the rounds concerns the Marine who had thrown several charges of TNT into a pillbox, but could still hear one Jap moving around. The Marine is supposed to have yelled, "Come on out and surrender, you Jap bastard!" And the Jap allegedly answered, "Go to hell, you souvenir-hunting Yankee son-of-a-bitch!"

0730: Back at Colonel Shoup's headquarters, his red-headed

operations officer, Major Tom Culhane, croaks happily, "We
got 'em by the eyeballs now!" Major Culhane has shouted orders over the telephone, above the din of battle, for nearly forty-
eight hours, until he sounds like Mr. Wendell Willkie shortly
after he opened his 1940 presidential campaign. Somebody
asked the major whether he thought his voice would last until
the battle ended. He answered, "I didn't think so last night,
but we are going so fast now I believe I'll finish in a whisper."

There is good news, too, about Major Rice and the rest of
the battalion staff I last saw as we started ashore. Major Rice's
amphtrack landed far up the beach and his men have been
fighting with Major Ryan's heroic piece of a battalion. Rice
himself has maintained communications for Ryan.

The single saddest tragedy on Betio is reported—not that one
American's death is sadder than any other, but because we
thought for a while this death might have been averted—Lieutenant Hawkins, the nonpareil Texan, died during the night.
One of the high-ranking officers comments in a low voice, "It's
not often that you can credit a first lieutenant with winning a
battle, but Hawkins came as near to it as any man could. He
was truly an inspiration."

Several officers sit under a palm tree. They have watched the
battle from its dark beginning to its present bright hopes of an
early end. Says Colonel Carlson, the old Marine Raider, "Did
you see three-eight (third battalion Eighth Marines) and one-
eight wading in? They were mowed down like flies. I believe
one-eight had a hundred casualties in less than a minute."

Said Colonel Edson, the hero of Guadalcanal, "This is the
first beachhead they have really defended. They had no choice
but to defend here—they had no interior position to retreat to;
it was all exterior. Anyway," he smiles, "it won't last as long as
Guadalcanal."

Captain "Frenchy" Moore, the Navy doctor who is division
surgeon, shakes his head. "I was on Guadalcanal. And it was
duck soup."

One of the officers off a transport comments, "I was at the Sicily landing. It was a pink-tea party, with ninety percent girls and ten percent boys."

Carlson: "This was not only worse than Guadalcanal. It was the damnedest fight I've seen in thirty years of this business."

It occurs to me that perhaps this Tarawa battle is going to be history, after all.

0800: Dr. Moore reports that six hundred wounded had been evacuated to the ships by last night, including four wounded who were floated out of a disabled tank lighter through a hole in its side. Up to now thirty-six have been buried at sea from the ships.

Preparations are being made for burying our own nearby dead, many of whom have been in the water for two days. It is a gruesome sight, even to men who have become hardened to anything, including the past two days' omnipresent sight and smell of death. Thirty-one Marines are now laid out in a line beyond the command post. Some are bloated, some have already turned a sickly green. Some have no faces, one's guts are hanging out of his body. The eyeballs of another have turned to a jellied mass, after so long a time in the water.

The corpsmen and burial parties continue to bring in the dead from the coral flats, now that those flats are subject to but little sniper fire. One dead American wears a soggy, blue, kapok life preserver—he probably cussed because all the rubber, inflating-type, life preservers had been passed out before his turn came. Here come four more waterlogged, lifeless bodies. All of them wear knives which they never got to use.

The bulldozer scoops a long trench, three feet deep. Its Seabee driver pays scant attention to the sniper who fires at him occasionally. The bodies, not even covered by a blanket or poncho, are brought over and placed in the trench, side by side, while Chaplains MacQueen and Kelly supervise their identification and last rites. This is no dignified burial—a man's last ceremony should be dignified, but this isn't. The bulldozer pushes some more dirt in the Marines' faces and that is all there is to it. Then the bulldozer starts digging a second trench.

Lines of corpsmen are bringing in the bodies as fast as they can find stretchers and wade into the shallow water. One Marine is brought in who has suffered the greatest indignity of all. His head has been blown off completely. His left arm is gone, and only a few shreds of skin hang from his shoulders. I thought I had become inured to anything, but I am nauseated by this sight. I turn to the big red-bearded Marine gunner who is standing beside me and say, "What a hell of a way to die!" The gunner looks me in the eye and says, "You can't pick a better way."

1000: For the first time a good view of the battle is available. There is a five-foot-high lumber pile beyond the incompleted barracks building. It is possible to stand behind this lumber and watch the battle that is being waged across the airfield and to the eastward—by now bombs and artillery and naval gunfire and mortars have sheared the fronds off most of the coconut palms, and Betio is nearly bare except for the stumps of the trees.

To the awful symphony of the big guns is added the crackling rifle fire of hundreds of Marines and several pillboxes full of well-hidden Japs. Marines dart across the expanse of the airfield while machine guns and snipers' rifles kick up dust around them. They dodge from shellhole to shellhole as they advance toward the enemy. One Marine is wounded but drags himself the remaining ten feet to a shellhole, where eager hands pull him out of further danger. On the other side of the runway a medium tank, looking like a great, clumsy bug, lumbers up to a pillbox and begins blasting away, from less than fifty feet, round after round of 75-mm. shells. A Jap, naked except for his white cloth G-string, runs out of the pillbox and throws himself under the tread of the tank. There is a small explosion as the Jap's hand grenade goes off, but his suicide nets him nothing except his idea of a warrior's heaven. The grenade does not even blow the tank's tread off. The tank lumbers over the Jap, still firing. Further down the field, Marines carrying mortar containers and boxes of ammunition walk across the open area. There are three of them. They do not even bother to try to run, though bullets spitting into the dust of the runway down this way plainly demonstrate that they are being fired at.

One of the destroyer shells finds a hitherto undiscovered oil dump in the middle of the island and the flames reach up very high. The destroyer gloatingly increases its firing until an area more than a hundred feet square is a roaring mass of flame and smoke. The island thumps and quivers, and flame and dust and curtains of smoke blend into the medley of unearthly noise.

1030: A dozen of us are standing around, or leaning against the big pillbox that protects Colonel Shoup's headquarters from frontal fire. All of a sudden a sniper who has apparently worked his way around to the side opens up. The bullets whiz through the command post, past the new ammunition dump we have started. Marines who are working on the dump start running. All of us at headquarters hit the dirt. All except rocklike Dave Shoup. He stands, fully exposed, arms akimbo, and bellows, "Stop! God damn it! What are you running for? Take cover, then move on up and kill the bastard." The Marines sheepishly work themselves back westward. One who was hit on the side of the face by a bullet is bandaged and led off.

Five prisoners, naked except for their split-toed shoes, are marched into headquarters by Captain John T. O'Neill of Somerville, Massachusetts, and two enlisted men armed with tommy guns. The prisoners sit around a coconut palm on their haunches, looking up and frowning curiously as if they wonder what on earth will happen to them. They are short, but well-muscled and apparently well-fed. Only one has been wounded; his left hand is bandaged. An intelligence officer questions them briefly in Japanese, then Colonel Shoup orders them sent out to the ship which is receiving prisoners. "Korean laborers," says the intelligence officer. "They are mighty glad to get captured."

A few minutes later another prisoner is led in, but this one, also a husky Korean, has been allowed to retain his short, civilian-gray pants. He wears a bandage on his neck, another on his arm. He tells the intelligence officer he had arrived on Betio only a few days ago—he had been cutting coconut logs on another island further up the atoll; these logs were shipped down to Betio, whose concealing foliage had been only slightly disturbed until the American battleships started working on it —D Day.

1130: Back of the incompleted barracks building is a big tinsmith shop. The sheets of tin and galvanized iron tell us that the Japs had plans to continue building up Betio. Many of the sheets are just so much twisted and perforated metal, but some are still serviceable. Of them the Marines build shelter from the noonday equatorial sun. Beside the mass of tin there is a big pile of twisted steel pipe. Marines who are bringing in more guns have trouble wheeling the 37's over it. Some of the Marines have already collected the long .303 Jap rifles. The newer rifles have a straight-shanked bayonet instead of the bayonet with the half loop at the hilt (for catching the enemy's bayonet and twisting his gun out of his hand). Japs on Attu and Guadalcanal had bayonets with loops at the hilt.

Along this area atop the seawall there are half-sunken machine-gun emplacements every five yards. These little coconut-log fortresses are shaped like a Y with the top half-closed, covered with sand which is covered by palm fronds. To look at row upon row of these pillboxes facing the sea, it seems impossible that the Marines ever got ashore D Day. But, in one of them, somewhat larger than most along here, I think I find the answer. Inside the pillbox there are four dead Japs and two dead Marines. Enough of those men in the first wave got ashore, jumped in with the Japs and killed them. Thus they knocked out enough machine guns so that others in later waves might live and win. Looking down on these two Marines, I can say, "These men gave their lives for me. I can understand it, because this machine gun covered the part of the water I had to wade through. They also gave their lives for one hundred and thirty million other Americans who realize it, I fear, only dimly." My feeling is one of deep humility and of respect for such brave men—God rest their souls. How much every man in battle owes to every other man! How easy to see on the battlefield that we are all in this thing together!

1200: The pillbox which contained the four Japs Lieutenant Doyle killed has been cleaned out. It is now a communication center, and a switchboard is functioning inside it. Lieutenant Charlie Lowry of Valdosta, Georgia, who has an 81-mm. mortar platoon, has stopped inside the log-barricaded entrance. "I've lost about a fourth of my men," he says. "That's just the number of casualties we've had," says George T. Olson of Jackson, Mississippi, staff sergeant of the regimental communicators. "Ten out of forty."

There is still some sniping, and a bullet whizzes overhead now and then. After one furious burst, Sergeant Olson says, "It doesn't do much good to duck unless you're in direct line of fire. You might duck the wrong way and get a stray bullet anyhow."

"You sure can tell the difference between new men and those who have been through it before," Olson continues. "One kid was shaking all over this morning because he had to cross the air strip. I didn't send him. But two of my men have been walking through the line of fire all day. They don't seem to mind it." Across the strip we could see from this rear entrance to the pillbox four ammunition carriers calmly walking along, as if they were strolling through Central Park, completely unmindful of a dozen popping machine guns, the crash of artillery and naval gunfire, and the pall of smoke and fire.

"This morning some of the natives were brought over from one of the other islands," says the sergeant. "They said the Japs had told their men a million Americans couldn't take Tarawa. I guess we are doing all right."

1230: In a shellhole with two Marines. Sniper fire is still rather severe—sometimes we surround a sniper, pass him, and assume somebody has killed him, when all of a sudden he lets go a flock of bullets. Then we cannot find him under his log or in his hole. One is shooting at something beyond us, and his soprano bullets sing over our heads. Says one grinning Marine, "I have only one regret—that John L. Lewis is not beside me." Says the other, "He wouldn't be alive if he was beside me. I don't mean the Japs would kill him. I would."

I had noticed this savage attitude toward labor grow steadily for a long time. It was particularly obvious during the bitter battle of Attu, which was fought during a coal strike. The man who is risking his life rarely stops to consider that there may be justice on the side of the striker, if such a thing is possible in wartime, or that other interests greedily force the laborer's cost of living toward an inflationary point. He simply figures that (1) a soldier gets fifty dollars a month for leading the most dangerous, most miserable life this side of hell, and (2) the laborer living in the faraway dream-world of the United States should be willing to forego a few extra cents an hour if it will help get material to the soldier to help him win the war. Only a man who has been on a battlefield can realize how wide is the maw of war. The amount of material required to fight a battle is probably beyond the civilian conception, the soldier figures. When the soldier sees how small a dent he and his comrades have made against the Japanese, and how much more material is necessary to win the Pacific war, he goes red-eyed at the mention of a strike. Oddly, the soldiers bitterest against labor are often labor-union members themselves.

To the soldier this is all a part of the gap between civilian conception of war and the realities of war—something the soldier himself does not bridge until he has been in a bloody, stinking, unromantic battle. He is likely to grow angry at the Army and Navy publicity men who are forever telling the folks back home how well Joe is treated. He gets mad at the "god-

damn U.S.O. soldiers" who are stationed safely in the United
States. He often scorns the newspapers and radio, particularly
those "rear-area people" who rewrite and pump up the drily
factual communiqué until it reads pretty and sparkles optimistically and sells more copies of the evening newspaper. The soldier wants the people back home to know that "we don't knock
hell out of 'em" every day of every battle. He wants the people
to understand that war is tough and war is horrible. He thinks
labor's tendency to strike is a part of this misconception on the
part of his own people at home—surely, no sane man would
dream of striking against his own soldiers if he understood what
war was like. I often speculate on whether or not labor did not
set itself back ten hard-won years in the last ten giddy months
of 1943, because I know labor will have one day to account to
some ten million angry men—minus those killed in action fighting labor's war.

1300: I haven't seen a man killed today.

1330: Back of the seawall, fifty yards farther westward than I
have ventured previously, nine dead Marines have been gathered from the interior of the island and placed in a row. Some
are covered with ponchos, some with a convenient palm frond.
Nearby there is a cheap, cardboard Japanese suitcase, its contents scattered. All the Jap civilian's underclothing and shirts
are silk. The shirt may have been captured. It is marked: "British produce—M. K. Mills. Size 36." Nearby there are thirteen
dead Jap soldiers, dressed in the green wool Navy Landing
Force uniform and wrap-around leggings such as U. S. soldiers
wore uncomfortably in World War I. Burial parties are beginning to bury the Japs a little farther inland, because the
smell of the dead is becoming overpowering after three days.
If any sign were needed that victory is ours, this is it: we have
started burying the Japs.

A light tank stops at a fuel dump and four grimy, black-faced
Marines hop out. The tank gunner is an Iowa farm boy named
Lowell Richman. I ask him how many Japs he has killed today

and he gives the modest Marine's answer, "I don't know." His pal says, "He's killed plenty. We are really knocking them off now." Says Richman, "We get 'em mostly by running up to the hole of the pillbox and dropping in some high explosive. If they run out we empty the canister into them."

A hundred yards farther up the beach I run into a conversation which has material in it for a sermon. Two Marines from the Third Battalion, Second Regiment, evidently old friends, are standing behind the seawall—there is considerable sniper fire hereabouts. One Marine is from Brooklyn, he tells me. He is fed up with the war. "I want to get back home now," he says. "I want to quit the Marines next year when I am nineteen— my four years will be up. I joined up because I didn't know any better and I stayed in because of patriotism—I got malaria at Guadalcanal and I could have gone home. But now I want to go stateside." His companion, another Iowa farm boy—he had married a New Zealand girl—attempted to quiet his friend, "Hell, if you don't stay out here and get shot at, somebody else will have to come out here and get shot at. Somebody's got to win the war. I could have gone back—I had malaria, too. But now I don't want to go back till it's over. You're not fighting just for yourself; you're fighting for the whole United States."

1400: It is quiet around this pillbox, although there is some fire two hundred yards ahead. Six medical corpsmen and a doctor use this pillbox for collecting the wounded, but they have not been busy this afternoon—not nearly as busy as when they arrived yesterday. One of them tells of a Marine from Utica, New York. He was wounded on D Day, shrapnel in his head, arms, and legs, as the amphtrack approached the shore. "Everybody in the amphtrack was killed except him and his buddy," says a corpsman, "and his buddy lasted only one day. Then he spent two and a half days in that amphtrack in the broiling sun. His eyes were clotted over, his throat scratched inside like a piece of tin. He tried to commit suicide last night, he was in such agony, but he was too weak to pull the trigger.

When we got to him he just said, 'Pour some water over my face, will you?' Plasma picked him up, and he's going to be all right, we think."

Said another corpsman, "These Marines don't complain when they are wounded. I certainly have got a lot of respect for them. I guess they must be the best fighting men in the world."

Outside, there was some discussion as to whether a dead man was a Jap or a Marine. He had been badly mutilated by shrapnel, and his body had turned a dark green. Most of his face had been blown off. He looked Japanese, but he wore Marine Corps outer clothing, "civvies" instead of the Jap G-string, and he had a lot of hair on his chest. Finally, the burial detail found his name on the inside of his belt, and took him away to be buried with the Americans.

The Japs around this pillbox, in this big hole, are bigger than any I have seen; three of the four are six feet tall and they are all heavy, even before bloating. The three dead Marines, who apparently had knocked out the pillbox and its machine gun, are about the same size. The sun has raised blisters as big as half dollars on the skin of brown men and white men alike.

Best unofficial estimate of our casualties: six hundred dead, twelve hundred wounded.

1500: Two concrete mixers evidence further the Japs' intention of holding Tarawa. Here is what looks like a fence made of steel grating, six feet high, surrounding a squared area on a concrete base. The Japs had got as far as installing the reinforcing steel, but they had not poured the concrete walls when we arrived. Here is a concrete bomb shelter, about twenty by thirty feet. Marines say there is a dead Jap officer inside. He apparently had been wounded two days ago, had crawled inside to die. They drag him out and search the tomb-like structure, finding boxes full of what appear to be pay-roll books and war-savings stamps. The walls of this shelter, which have barely been nicked by bombs and shells, measure fifty-five inches thick.

1530: From behind the bomb shelter we can see a half-track fifty yards ahead working on a Jap pillbox. The Marines pour round after round of 75-mm. shells into the entrance of the pillbox. Five or six Japs run out, straight into the withering heat of a flamethrower that is waiting for them.

These Marines are from the first battalion of the Eighth, which took such heavy casualties in the water yesterday morning. Pfc. James Collins of Spartanburg, South Carolina, recalls, "The water was red with blood. All around me men were screaming and moaning. I never prayed so hard in all my life. Only three men out of twenty-four in my boat ever got ashore that I know of." Collins carried one wounded man back to the Higgins boat. Then he started back with another, a corpsman who had been hit in the shoulder. On the way the corpsman was hit again, half his head blown off while Collins held him in his arms. A preliminary check shows that B Company got ninety men ashore out of 199. Pfc. William Coady of Minersville, Pennsylvania, says he carried ten wounded men back to the Higgins boat before he finally made shore. A Marine from the regimental weapons platoon says his outfit didn't fare so badly—only one man had been killed and two wounded out of thirty-six.

1730: Major General Julian Smith has arrived from the battleship on which he maintained headquarters with Admiral Hill—but, even on the third day, the Japs kept a sharp lookout for new arrivals. The general's amphtrack, which also contained two brigadier generals, was fired upon as it rounded the west end of the island, and its driver was wounded. Rumors, later proved exaggerated, are prevalent, even at headquarters. One officer reports that only 140 men remain out of the first and second battalions of the Eighth Marines, and that more than fifty percent of the officers have been killed or wounded out of the six assaulting battalions which faced enemy fire as they came in.

1800: By now all the war correspondents are accounted for. Keith Wheeler of the Chicago *Times* and John Henry of I.N.S.

reached headquarters today after landing yesterday to the west, their amphtrack having been turned back the first day, causing them to spend a night bobbing around in the lagoon. It is a miracle that none of the civilian correspondents was killed *— they are the only "unit" which has suffered no casualties. Not one of the newsmen who accompanied the assault battalions as they waded ashore failed to see men killed around him. It is comforting to know that they all came through Tarawa, the toughest of them all, because in two years I have lost friends and colleagues all the way from New Guinea and Australia to Berlin.

But few war correspondents have experienced the horror which Gil Bundy, the artist, went through on his first assignment. He got into a landing boat with some of the regimental command on D Day. Bundy's boat received a direct hit about seventy-five yards from shore, probably from a Jap 90-mm. mortar. All others in it were killed or blown out of the boat, but Bundy miraculously was unharmed. That was only the beginning of his troubles. He jumped from his disabled boat, intending to swim to another boat. But a swift current carried him several hundred yards out to sea. Finally, he managed to pull up panting to another disabled boat. Several dead men were in it, but by then it was dark and Bundy had no choice but to spend the night with the dead Marines. Early on the morning of the second day a boat which was returning from the beach stopped by Bundy's morgue. Captain Harry Lawrence of Albany, Georgia, the officer in charge of the amphtrack company, almost shot Bundy for a Jap—during the night Japs had swum out and manned some of the amphtracks. Bundy, rescued, was taken back to a transport. Until today we had assumed that Bundy had been killed. His identification papers had been found in his original boat, and several Marines had reported having seen his lifeless body, as men in battle often report things they are ninety percent certain of.

* Two Marine Corps correspondents were killed: Lieutenant Ernest A. Matthews, Jr., of Dallas, and Staff Sergeant Wesley L. Kroenung of South Pasadena.

1830: Two-thirds of the island's area is now ours. Lieutenant
Commander Fabian, the beachmaster charged with unloading
the hundreds of tons of supplies now pouring over the pier,
says, yes, he thinks he knows the quickest way to get to a nearby
ship which might lend the reporters typewriters. Wading
through enemy fire carrying a typewriter is not standard pro-
cedure for war correspondents, who are usually dependent on
the Navy for the loan of materials. Mr. Fabian introduces me
and Dick Johnston and Keith Wheeler to a transport skipper,
Captain Claton McLaughlin, who says, "Sure, come with me.
I'm just returning to my ship."

The ship is a new AK—part transport, part cargo ship. The
ship's crew is anxious for news of the battle. They grin when
they hear that the last round is beginning. Says a sailor, "I'd
have given anything in the world if I could have been over
there on land to help out." The young junior-grade lieutenant
who is the ship's supply officer opens up his ship's store to pro-
cure razors, tooth brushes, and soap. He will not accept pay—
one of the correspondents had somehow retained some money.
"It's the first time I've had a chance to do anything, and the battle only two thousand yards away," he says, bitterly. In the ward
room the hovering Negro mess steward brings in extra, after-
hours helpings of ham and iced tea and coffee. The captain
turns over his quarters to the correspondents, including a
blessed fresh-water shower bath (but it will take many baths to
purge the grime of Betio from the skin pores). The yeoman in
the ship's office finds typewriters and onion-skin paper which is
necessary to take the many carbon copies the rules say a correspondent must turn in.

This desire to lend a helping hand is one of the most touch-
ing things in and around a battle, where every man wants to
help every other man. I have seen men, when asked for a cigarette, feel the inside of the pack, find only one left. They bulge
out the pack, proffer the last cigarette, then pocket the empty
pack so the other man will not know that he is accepting the

last one. On Betio the drinking water is almost undrinkable—the five-gallon cans had been filled in New Zealand many weeks before and the heat of the South Pacific had caused some of the enamel lining to dissolve into the water. Thus, the only palatable water was that which each man brought in his two canteens from his transport. Yet I have seen several men give their last drink of water to a comrade, with the untrue remark, "Oh, I've got some more in my other canteen." What a pity Americans at home cannot display the same unselfish attitude toward each other and toward the men who fight for them!

Within an hour after the correspondents left the island the Japs staged their twilight counterattack. All day Major Bill Jones' first battalion of the Sixth Marines had marched gallantly down the south shore of Betio. The tanks went down the beach first, except for those incredibly brave Marines who went ahead and spotted for the tanks. The tanks poured high explosives into the seaward openings of the mighty coconut log and sand pillboxes. Then the Marine riflemen fired into those openings to kill whatever Japs were left. The flamethrowers did the rest. By dusk the Sixth had been able to travel slightly more than halfway down the south shore. There the Marines dug in for the night, with wounded Captain Krueger's Company B, now in command of Lieutenant Norman K. Thomas, holding the front line. The Japs from the tail end of the island, despite three days of merciless pounding, were able to stage their *"Banzai!"* attack. Having cautiously stayed hidden in their holes for three days, the emperor-worshiping brown men now threw away all caution in anticipation of inevitable death. Screaming "Marine, you die!" and "Japanese drink Marines' blood!" they rushed Company B in what seemed like overpowering numbers. The line wavered, and in one place it cracked momentarily. Lieutenant Thomas telephoned Major Jones, "We are killing them as fast as they come at us, but we can't hold much longer; we need reinforcements." Said Jones, "We haven't got them to send you; you've got to hold." Company B held. At least three hundred Japs died in their fanatical charge. Company B's feat was one of the most heroic on Betio. The red-eyed, grime-coated Marines who stumbled out of the front line next morning, more dead than alive, muttered, "They told us we had to hold . . . and, by God, we held." That line, I reflected, might be added to the Marine Corps hymn.

The rest of the night passed without incident beyond Washing Machine Charley's nocturnal prowl. Aboard Captain McLaughlin's ship General Quarters sounded about 0230. Said a sailor, "Don't let this bother you, but we all hope Charley doesn't aim at the island and hit us. A hell of a lot of our cargo is bombs and hundred-octane gasoline." The Jap bombing accuracy was often the subject of American amusement at this funny-war: "I don't want to be here when the airport gets ready. The Japs will come over and bomb and aim for the airport and hit you in the tail way down at the other end of the island."

was late afternoon of the fourth day before I finished writing and got ashore again. As I walked up the pier, from the comparatively clean-smelling sea, the overwhelming smell of the dead hit me full in the face, and I vomited a little. By dark I was used to it again.

That fourth night Dick Johnston and I spent on the south shore of the island, in a tank trap with Major Rice, who had by now become, at twenty-five, probably the youngest battalion commander in the Marine Corps; his operations officer, Captain Ben Owens; the executive officer of the heavy-weapons company, Captain Bill Tynes; and the battalion adjutant, Lieutenant Albert Borek. Said Borek, "I'm afraid to tell you what the battalion casualties were. The best count I can get is 309 men left out of 750 who landed. There are fifteen officers left out of thirty-nine."

Said Ben Owens, "We were talking about medals. We decided nobody should be recommended because everybody should have one."

VIEW OF THE CARNAGE

BETIO HAD BEEN DECLARED "secured" at 1312 on the fourth day, seventy-five hours and forty-two minutes after the first Marines hit the beach. Occasional snipers would fire from holes and rubble-and-corpse-packed pillboxes for days afterward. Until the battle ended I had covered only a small part of the island—perhaps a total of four hundred yards along the beach, and no more than one hundred yards inland. To understand what had happened in each sector, it was necessary to walk over the island yard by yard. This I did for a day and a half before I flew out of the lagoon on a PB2Y on the afternoon of the sixth day.

What I saw on Betio was, I am certain, one of the greatest works of devastation wrought by man. Words are inadequate to describe what I saw on this island of less than a square mile. So are pictures—you can't smell pictures.

So that the reader may be able to place the scenes I describe in their approximate positions, I have inserted three drawings of the three trips I made over Betio. (See p. 124.)

Here on the south beach the coconut-log and sand and concrete pillboxes are larger and more powerfully constructed than on the beach we invaded. Undoubtedly, the Japs, who had

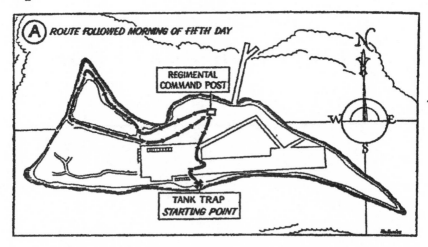

themselves landed on the north beach, expected us to land
there, and not through the lagoon. In the water there are rows
of land mines and double fences of barbed wire. There are fifteen dead Japs in and around the first pillbox next to the tank
trap, all dressed in green uniforms, wrap-around leggings, and
hobnailed shoes except one who wore a Navy flyer's blue uniform. Two of the fifteen have blown their guts out with hand
grenades, as evidenced by their missing stomachs and right
hands. Most of the bodies are already turning a sickly green,
though they have been corpses only two days—as against five for
most of the five thousand putrefying bodies on Betio.

Down the beach, it is possible to see these mighty fortresses,
one after another, as far as the eye can reach. There are twelve
Japs inside the second pillbox—more than the smaller machine-
gun boxes on the north shore could contain—and there are thirteen outside. Some of these wear only shorts, some only the
G-string shorts which do not cover the flanks.

After a brief alert, caused by friendly planes, which we spend
in a foxhole on the beach, Dick Johnston and I start across the
airstrip toward the regimental command post near the northern
shore. On the edge of the airstrip we find that the huge, fifteen-

foot-high, box-like structures made of coconut logs are not block-houses, but revetments to contain two planes. All the bombing and shelling have blown a few logs off these three-sided pens (the open side faces toward the runway), but generally they are surprisingly intact. There are perhaps a dozen Jap planes—Zeros and twin-engined bombers—along the runway, but only two inside the revetments which are fairly well riddled by shrapnel and bullets. The first light, maneuverable Zero we examine is in fairly good condition, however. The red ball of the Japanese is painted on both sides of the fuselage just back of the cockpit and on the top and bottom near each end of the wings.

A bullet-riddled, brown truck is on the edge of the runway. Inside the next big coconut-log revetment there are three identical trucks. Though they are Japanese-made, the dashboards of the trucks have their instruments labeled in English. Here is an example of the Japanese tendency to imitate: the "water" thermometer dial is in the centigrade of the French, as is the "kilos" of the speedometer; "oil" and "amperes" dials might have been taken from either the Americans or the British, but the fuel indicator is labeled "gasoline" instead of the British "petrol." The tires on this truck are four different brands: Dunlop, Bridgestone, Yokohama, and Firestone. An uncamouflaged black sedan nearby, also of Japanese make, had been hit and burned until there is less than half of it left. It has a license plate with the Navy anchor insignia on it, and the number $\frac{7}{233}$. The black-out oilcloth over the headlights has no ordinary little hole through which a small beam of light might show; it has a Navy anchor, which gives the headlights the appearance of a Hallowe'en pumpkin.

Beside one of the revetments four naked Marines take a bath in a well of brackish water. The well, many years old, had been there before the Japs came. It had gone through the Battle of Betio unharmed.

At headquarters Captain J. L. Schwabe, one of the regimental staff officers, says we will find at the northwest tip of the island (the bird's beak) spots where our flamethrowers killed thirty and forty Japs at a time. He estimates that 250 Marines were killed in the water along the north beach between headquarters and the beak. Estimates of casualties in the Second Regiment are sickening: First Battalion 63 killed, 192 wounded, 41 missing; Second Battalion has 309 left out of 750 who landed; Third Battalion has 413 left, about the same as Major Crowe's Second Battalion of the Eighth. These figures were found later to be somewhat exaggerated, but they indicate how forcefully the first casualty compilations struck us. Five cemeteries have been started thus far—by 0800 of the fifth day—and less than one-fourth of our dead have been buried. The largest cemetery, next to the regimental command post, has 134 graves; the others 80, 53, 20, and 41 respectively.

A bandy-legged little Korean who wears white cotton pants and golf stockings is trying to talk to the M.P.'s who are taking him to an interpreter. He is trying to tell the M.P.'s how many were on the island. He says "Nippon" and draws "6000" in the sand; then he says "Korean" and draws "1000."

Going westward up the beach, beyond the farthest point I had yet reached, we see on the beach the bodies of Marines who have not yet been reached by the burial parties. The first is a husky boy who must have been three inches over six feet tall. He was killed ten feet in front of the seawall pillbox which was his objective. He is still hunched forward, his rifle in his right hand. That is the picture of the Marine Corps I shall always carry: charging forward. A bit further up the beach there are four dead Marines only a few feet apart; ten feet along, another; fifteen feet further another; then there are six bunched together. These men, we are told, are from I and K companies of the Third Battalion, Second Regiment.

Fifty feet further up the beach, ten Marines were killed on the barbed wire on the coral flats. One of them was evidently shot as he placed his foot on the top rung of the wire—his trouser leg was caught on the barbs and the leg still hangs in the air. There are eighty more dead Marines scattered in a twenty-foot square of the beach just beyond. Six more . . . two more . . . four more. Here four got to the very mouth of the coconut-log pillbox, but none of them made it, because there are no dead Japs inside. But in the next pillbox there are two Japs sprawled over their machine gun, and in the next, five yards further along the seawall, there are three. All appear to have been killed by hand grenades.

We detour inland a few yards. Here, perhaps thirty feet back of the seawall, four Marines lie dead outside a larger pillbox. There are six dead Japs inside. Still thirty feet further inland three dead Japs lie inside another pillbox, and there are three Marines lying around the pillbox. It is not difficult to see that the Marines were determined to keep on killing Japs while the breath of life remained in them, whether that last breath was drawn in the water, at the barricade, or at some undetermined point inland. What words can justify such bravery in the face of almost certain death? They died, but they came on. Those machine guns were killing other Marines out in the water, and who ever heard of one Marine letting another down?

Here Amphtrack Number 15—name: "Worried Mind"—is jammed against the seawall. Inside it are six dead Marines; next to it are three more. Two more lie impaled on the barbed wire next to the twenty-eight-seater Jap privy over the water. Their clothing ties them to the wire. They float at anchor. A half dozen Marines, members of the engineer regiment, are walking around the beach, examining the bodies. "Here's Larson," says one. "Here's Montague," says another. The bodies, as they are identified, are tenderly gathered up and taken fifteen or twenty yards inland, where other Marines are digging graves for them.

This is unusual, because most of the Marines are being gathered up by burial parties, which have not progressed this far. But these men are looking for the dead from their own particular company. Since they are leaving by transport in a few hours, I suppose they think: "Here is the last thing we can do for these boys we have known so long. We'll do it with our own hands."

When I passed that way again several hours later, the Eighteenth Marines had gone, had sailed away. But I noticed the fifteen graves this particular company had dug. A rude cross had been erected over each grave—undoubtedly replaced later by a neat white cross—and on the cross had been written the name of the Marine who lay underneath it, the designation that he was a Marine, and the date of his death, thus:

A. R. Mitlick
U.S.M.C.
20-11-43

In front of the fifteen graves, so that all would know which outfit they came from, and that they all came from D Company of the Eighteenth, the Marines had proudly erected a larger cross:

3-2-18

The names of these fifteen, right to left, were: R. C. McKinney, G. G. Seng,* R. C. Kountzman, R. L. Jarrett, Max J. Lynnton, C. Montague,* S. P. Parsons, M. W. Waltz, H. H. Watkins, H. B. Lanning, J. S. Castle, A. B. Roads, A. R. Mitlick, W. A. Larson, and R. W. Vincent, First Lieutenant.

Just behind the coconut-log wall where the men of D Company had died there is a pit containing a 77-mm. gun, whose ammunition supply had been half exhausted. A few yards further along the wall there is a 13-mm. machine gun. Inside the gun pit is a half-pint bottle of the only brand of whisky I have

---

* Gene Seng and Charlie Montague, aged twenty-one, had been childhood friends. They had gone to school together in Texas. On February 3, 1942, they had volunteered for the Marines together. On November 20, 1943, on Tarawa, they died together.

ever seen in Japanese possession. The label, like the labels of many Japanese commercial products, is in English:

Rare Old Island Whisky

SUNTORY

First Born in Nippon

Choicest Products

Kotobukiya Ltd.

Bottled at our own Yamazaki Distillery

A Marine near the gun pit had evidently been hit squarely by a 77-mm. shell (77 mm. is about three inches). There is a hole through his midsection, and he is badly burned—so badly that he could hardly be identified as a Marine but for the laced leggings under his trouser legs. A Marine who is standing nearby, Pfc. Glenn Gill of Oklahoma, explains that the remnants of the first and second waves of 3/2 rushed over the barricade, where they were pinned down as the third wave got all the machine-gun attention.

A hundred yards inland we find an air-raid sound detector, which is sandbagged all around, and a power plant, which was protected only by a tin roof that was smashed to a thousand pieces. There are wooden-compartmented boxes full of carpenter's tools and some more delicate instruments. Next to the power plant there is a thirty-six-inch searchlight, and in the middle of a group of buildings and pillboxes a hole ten feet deep, twenty feet in diameter. The sixteen-inch shell or one-thousand-pound bomb which made that hole could not have fallen anywhere else within a hundred yards without destroying something. Near the shellhole there are two Japs blown completely in two. Only the lower extremities of either are anywhere in sight—one was cut in two at the waist, the other at the hips. In a smaller shellhole there are six dead Japs around a 77-mm. gun—this had once been a Jap gun pit. On the rim of the gun pit lies a dead Marine, who looks as if he might have been killed while diving in. Another 77-mm. gun—they are very thick along this northwest beach—has been knocked out by shellfire. The barrel is splintered and twisted. In a bomb crater there are fourteen Japs, evidently tossed in there by Marines cleaning out pillboxes before inhabiting them. Another 77-mm. gun has not been touched by shellfire, but the eight Japs in the pit were killed by rifle fire.

Amphtrack Number 48 is jammed against the seawall barricade. Three waterlogged Marines lie beneath it. Four others are scattered nearby, and there is one hanging on the two-foot-high strand of barbed wire who does not touch the coral flat at all. Back of the 77-mm. guns there are many hundreds of rounds of 77-mm. ammunition.

At the tip of the Betio bird's beak, there is the first big Jap gun I have seen: 5.5 inches. It is set in a concrete cup, and the degrees of the compass are painted on the rim of the cup. Shells for the gun, which are about twenty inches long, are contained in six little compartments, six shells to a compartment, inside the walls of the cup. Outside the cup there are hundreds more shells. The gun turret has been hit by about fifty fifty-caliber strafing bullets which probably also killed the gun crew, who have been removed, but otherwise the gun is untouched.

Turning southward up the Betio bird's forehead, we find another 5.5-inch gun thirty yards away. Shells or bombs have nicked the inside of its cup at 170 degrees, 220 degrees, and 30 degrees. The four Japs inside the pit have been charred to sticks of carbon.

Outside the gun emplacement a dog, suffering from severe shell shock, wanders drunkenly. When some Marines whistle and call him he trembles and tries to run, but falls. Not far away there is a placid cat with a dirty red ribbon around his neck. A sergeant of an engineer platoon calls the roll of his outfit, which arrived late and had only one man wounded. But its flame-throwers killed dozens of the reeling Japs.

The pillboxes here along the west beach, spaced only ten feet apart, are connected by trenches. Near another 77-mm. gun there is another 36-inch searchlight. Like all seven searchlights on Betio, this one was a favorite target of strafing planes, and all were destroyed. Between this 77-mm. gun and another similar gun thirty yards up the beach the Japs have pointed a coconut log out to sea. To a pilot five hundred feet in the air it could very well be mistaken for a six-inch gun.

About halfway up the west beach we turn inland and start back through the center of the island, past the body of a bloated Jap officer lying next to more dull-brown trucks. A bit further toward the center, the Marines have thrown a few shovelfuls of sand over the ghastly, mangled bodies of a dozen Japs. Dead Japs are strewn liberally along the road that leads through the center, eight here, two there, thirty over there where they were caught by a flamethrower. Two lie beside a Jap light tank, which is camouflaged in the navy fashion of World War I. On the other side of the tank lies a Marine, whose body's site is marked for burial parties by the age-old method; his bayoneted rifle jabbed upright into the ground.

Here was a Jap warehouse, which burned to the ground at least three days ago. It was filled apparently with foodstuffs, mostly canned: salmon, shrimp, rice. Whoever dreams of starving out Japs should know that they always have enough food to last many months, not counting fish that they can catch, birds that they can kill, and coconuts they can pick. Near the warehouse there are the mangled remains of a dozen bicycles, of which the Japs must have had a thousand on Betio, in addition to perhaps a hundred cars and trucks, and great quantities of miniature rail equipment. Further on there are bales of sacks labeled in English: "Stores Government—Stores Department." Great stacks of cases of rifle ammunition have not been touched by the terrific bombardment. A Seabee walks out of a pillbox with a fencing costume that looks like a baseball catcher's equipment: a steel face mask and a "belly protector" made of laced

bamboo and heavy blue cloth. Scattered along the road are several one-man sniper pits: gasoline drums sunk into the ground,
with a lid for cover.

Between the road and the north beach, spaced some fifty yards
apart, there are three big coconut-log bomb shelters, about
twenty by fifty feet inside. Outside they are covered on the top
and on the sides by three to ten feet of sand. None was touched
either by aerial or naval bombardment. The occupants, cower-
ing in their corners, had been killed by TNT and flamethrowers. A Marine intelligence officer tells his sergeant to tell his
men to search the bodies for documents. "Sir, don't ask them
to," pleads the sergeant. "They are puking already."

A tank trap has been constructed diagonally across the section
of the island north of the runway that forms part of the air-strip
triangle. It is a long, deep ditch whose sides are braced by upright coconut logs. Nearby there is another twenty-by-fifty bomb
shelter, which is reinforced concrete inside, tiers of coconut logs
in the middle and sand on the outside covered by palm fronds.
I wonder: would the heaviest bomb ever made tear up this unbelievable fortification? Or if the bomb hit on the rounded sides
of the blockhouse, would it not glance off and explode harmlessly alongside the blockhouse? Several bomb holes around the
sides of the blockhouse indicate that "near misses" do no good.

Another burned warehouse contains hundreds of bottles of
sake, most of them broken. Also stacks of uniforms, hundreds
of pots and pans, several gross of little blue enamelware cereal
bowls and cups with the Navy anchor stenciled on them, about
eighty bicycles, and a number of pressure cookers. Like other
navies, the Japanese Navy apparently is far more luxuriously
equipped than the Army.

By 1030 the Seabees are working like a thousand beavers on
the airfield, which must be prepared quickly in order that the
Americans on Betio will have fighter protection. Actually, there
is not a great deal for them to do before planes can land. The
main runway, along the longitudinal center of the island, is con-

crete and it is in almost perfect condition. The shorter runways, of gravel, are almost as well preserved. The planes and ships had orders to lay off the runways. If their accuracy was such that they could lay off specified areas, then why could they not hit the targets assigned to them? The Seabees, many of them skilled workmen old enough to be the fathers of most of the Marines, are having a great time. Little, rubber-tired Jap carts provide much amusement for Seabees who wheel supplies up and down the runways with them. One Seabee boasts that his outfit has already killed two Jap snipers this morning.

More evidence of the care the Japs had used in building up Betio: an unharmed gasoline truck sunk into an underground revetment, a twelve-by-thirty concrete water storage tank, still three-quarters filled with water, another big warehouse—the battleships and bombers really tore up the unprotected warehouses, two black automobiles, three more destroyed buildings.

Two hundred yards west of the regimental command post there is an American graveyard which by now contains seventy Marines, and seven more bodies lie on the ground awaiting burial. The first grave is marked, on a crude piece of packing-case lumber, "Unidentified." Other names I note at random: Lieutenant Colonel David K. Claude,* J. F. Svoboda, Duffy, Jenkins, P. L. Olano, W. R. Jay, W. A. Carpenter, M. D. Dinnis, C. E. McChee, W. C. Culp, F. R. Erislip, W. H. Soeters, "Unknown," L. N. Carney, Hicks, R. E. Bemis, E. R. Pero, C. J. Hubarski, H. Schempf.

Before I returned to regimental (now division) headquarters, the corps commander of the Gilbert Islands assaults (i.e., both Makin and Tarawa) had arrived: Major General Holland McTyeire Smith, one of the most colorful figures in the Marine Corps. Alabama-born Holland Smith is the father of amphibious training of U. S. armed forces. Many years ago he foresaw that

* Later that day someone remarked, "I wonder where Colonel Claude is. I haven't seen him in two days." Colonel Claude was an observer from another division, unattached to any particular outfit. He was killed up front with the Scout and Sniper Platoon.

one day it would be necessary for American soldiers and Marines to land on enemy beaches in the face of hostile fire. In awarding him the Distinguished Service Medal, Navy Secretary Frank Knox had said of him: "He laid the groundwork for amphibious training of practically all American units, including at various times the First and Third Marine Divisions, the First, Seventh, and Ninth Infantry Divisions of the Army and numerous other Marine Corps and Army personnel. His proficient leadership and tireless energy in the development of high combat efficiency among the forces under his supervision were in keeping with the highest traditions of the United States Naval Service."

Nonetheless, Holland Smith, beloved by the Marine Corps, had assumed the aspects of a barnacle, so far as much of the regular Navy was concerned. He spoke his mind whenever he saw something wrong, even if that something were a brain child of his own. And in the regular Navy the first rule is to speak softly, particularly if the speech contains something that might not reflect credit on everybody else. Holland Smith at sixty-one was a military liberal, which few men in the U. S. Navy dare to be after fifty.

I had known General Smith a long time, in San Diego where he was training amphibious forces, on Attu, on Kiska, aboard a transport, a battleship, and a couple of airplanes. Because he was an unusual major general, he was delightful, and I was glad to see him. Although his route over the western end of the island duplicated some of the territory I had covered in the morning, I looked forward to listening to his comments on an inspection during the afternoon, along with his Tarawa division commander, Julian Smith, his aide Major Clifton A. Woodrum, Jr., and two newsmen who had accompanied him by plane from Makin, Bernard McQuaid of the Chicago *Daily News* and Robert Trumbull of the New York *Times*. Said one of the newsmen —I forget which—"I guess we had a pretty tame show on Makin, compared to what the Marines had here." On Makin the 165th New York Infantry—the onetime "Fighting Sixty-Ninth"—had found about 250 Japs, plus some Korean laborers. In exterminating them, the 165th had had 65 killed, 121 wounded. "A lot of our casualties were caused by the wild firing of our men"—but that was not news; it always happens when green troops go into battle. The 165th had had the misfortune to lose its colonel, Gardiner Conroy, who was killed by a Jap sniper.

Before the tour started there was, at Julian Smith's suggestion, a double flag-raising near headquarters; U. S. and British flags went up on twin flagpoles. There had been a devil of a time finding a British flag. Finally, Major Frank Lewis George Holland, who had been schoolmaster of the Gilberts before he was forced to flee when the Japs came, produced a British flag about half the size of the Stars and Stripes. In the words of Henry Keys, the Australian correspondent representing the London *Daily Express*, "Major Holland looked in his bag. It contained one pair of drawers and the Union Jack."

The generals' tour of the island started from headquarters southward, then west on the south shore, down the western end, then eastward along the northern shore:

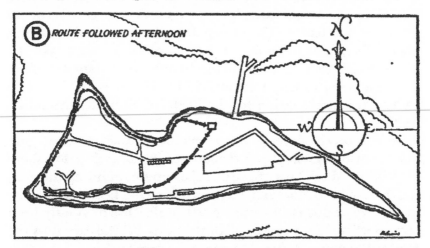

The first three dead men the generals see are Marines; one near a disabled Jap tank on the edge of the runway, two more

in a shellhole not far away. Fifty yards before they reach the
south shore, after crossing the runway, they find the hastily
scooped graves of three more Marines. I note the casualty tag
on one grave: "W. F. Blevins, Killed in Action, 11-22-43." Nearby
there is the lone grave of "Pvt. J. M. Redman, Killed in Action,
11-23-43." His helmet hangs on the cross, a bullet hole through
the center of it. A Marine near the south beach reports that some
'of his buddies killed Japs in a machine-gun nest over there only
three hours ago. And there are still snipers scattered throughout
the island that the Marines just can't find. "Uh-huh," uh-huhs
Holland Smith, who carries a carbine slung from his shoulder.

"There was one thing that won this battle, Holland," says
Julian Smith, "and that was the supreme courage of the Marines.
The prisoners tell us that what broke their morale was not the
bombing, not the naval gunfire, but the sight of Marines who
kept coming ashore in spite of their machine-gun fire. The Jap
machine-gun fire killed many Marines in the water and on the
beach. But other Marines came behind those who died. They
landed on the beaches, they climbed the seawall, and they went
into those enemy defenses. The Japs never thought we would
get to those defenses. They never thought they would lose this
island. They told their men a million of us couldn't take it."
Julian Smith tells Holland Smith about Lieutenant Hawkins,
that he is going to name the airfield for Hawkins. "His will be
my first recommendation for the Medal of Honor," says Julian
Smith.

On the beach there is a twin-mount 5.5-inch seacoast gun,
which obviously had been demounted from a ship for shore
duty. Three dead Japs are inside the cup surrounding the gun,
and there are two more in a cut-back which has been hit directly.
In the area of this twin-mount naval gunfire has obviously been
very effective. On a sand hill thirty yards behind the guns the
Japs had mounted a fire director and range finder.

A hundred yards or so west of the first guns there is another twin-mount 5.5-inch set of guns. This is a grisly sight. There are two Japs under the gun barrels who have committed suicide with hand grenades. Four· more are in a ditch leading from a nearby dugout. Only one of these is a suicide, but another's heart bulges out of his chest, which apparently has been rent open by a shell, and a third is only a stick of char.

The generals marvel at the strength of the machine-gun emplacements on this south shore—almost a solid wall of apparently impregnable defenses all the way up to the southwest tip of the island. They concede that one-six must have done a thoroughgoing job.

At the southwest tip of the island they see two of the four eight-inch guns which the Japs had on Betio. Both guns are pointed toward the direction from which our transports approached, but it is obvious that they were put out of action by some of the first salvos fired by our battleships. Hardly a round of eight-inch shells has been fired. It is easy to see what did the trick: a direct hit on the concrete powder chamber next to the guns. A gaping hole through the powder chamber indicates that a sixteen-inch shell perforated there. Inside the chamber there are about twenty-five charred Japs. Others are hanging on the jagged edge of the hole and for fifty yards beyond the hole Japs are spewed out over the sandy terrain. That must have been the terrific explosion we saw on the third battleship shot.

Next to the exploded powder chamber is the biggest hole on the pockmarked island of Betio—some sixty feet in diameter and much deeper than the sub-surface water level of the island. Scattered about the rim of the great hole are about two hundred rounds of eight-inch ammunition, evidence that the ammunition dump as well as the powder house blew up.

These two guns were served by a small mechanical trolley whose tracks circle the inside of the gun emplacements. The guns are labeled V. S. and M. (Vickers), indicating that they were captured from the British, or purchased from the British when

Japan was an ally. Both eight-inch guns have been hit directly many times. The smaller guns, notably 77-mm. and machine guns, might escape hits from the terrific bombing and shelling which preceded our attack, but the larger ones were comparatively easy targets.

The generals and their inspecting party turn north and head back from the Betio bird's tufted head toward its beak. They see what had been a Japanese radar screen, mounted on a concrete pedestal. In front of a sign—"Danger: Mines"—battle-weary Marines are swimming nude, attempting to wash the crust, the scum, and the odors of Betio from their tanned bodies. There are no dead bodies on the western end of the island to impede the swimming. The generals note the lone grave of Captain Thomas Royster of the Second Amphibious Tractor Battalion. As they pass two of the deadly 77-mm. guns which are still in working condition, Julian Smith remarks, "These are the guns that kill our people; we can knock out the big guns."

Three pigs lie in a pen. One of them is dead from shrapnel hits. The other two act dazed, merely grunt.

The Generals Smith examine a 13-mm. machine gun at the northwest tip of Betio. Hundreds of empty shells show that it was fired many times before the nearby Jap had the top of his head blown off. "That gun killed a lot of Marines," says Julian Smith.

When we reach the northern shore—the bird's throat—we notice an amazing phenomenon: the full tide is now washing against the seawall to a depth of three feet, and the Marines who were lying on the beach this morning are now floating against the seawall. In other words, the tide during those first two critical days was exceptionally low, perhaps due to a wind from the south, or the Marines would have had no beachhead at all! This was truly an Act of Providence.

The Marines floating in the water are now pitiful figures. Many of them have had the hair washed off their heads by this time. Julian Smith orders an additional burial party formed tc speed up the interment of the Americans. The eyes of the two veteran major generals are misty when they view the bodies of gallant Marines who were killed just before they reached the seawall. Says Holland Smith, "You must have three or four hundred here, Julian." But the most stirring sight is the Marine who is leaning in death against the seawall, one arm still supported upright by the weight of his body. On top of the seawall, just beyond his upraised hand, lies a blue and white flag, a beach marker to tell succeeding waves where to land. Says Holland Smith, "How can men like that ever be defeated? This Marine's duty was to plant that flag on top of the seawall. He did his duty, though it cost him his life. *Semper fidelis* meant more to him than just a catch phrase." We pass on down the seawall rather quickly, because it is impossible to look at such a sight, and realize its implications, without tears.

Three dead Japs lie in a pillbox behind the seawall. Near one of them there is a green-covered bound volume of the *National Geographic* for September-December, 1931, with markings in Japanese on the ends. The first article in the volume is about New Hampshire. Says New Hampshire-born Barney McQuaid, sticking the volume under his arm, "I am not ordinarily a souvenir-hunter, but, gentlemen, this is my souvenir."

The generals are awestruck when they inspect the pillboxes the assault troops had to knock out. "By God," says Holland Smith, "those Marines just kept coming. Many of them were killed, but more came on. It looks beyond the realm of a human being that this place could have been taken. These Japanese were masters of defensive construction. I never saw anything like these defenses in the last war. The Germans never built anything like this in France. No wonder these bastards were sitting back here laughing at us! They never dreamed the Marines could take this island, and they were laughing at what would happen to us when we tried it."

Back at headquarters there is the first complete report on what happened on the other twenty-four islands of the Tarawa Atoll. The Second Battalion of the Sixth Infantry had landed on the next island, Bairiki, where a few Japs offered light resistance. But most of them fled to Abaokora, northernmost island of the atoll, with the Marines pursuing hotly. From there the Japs could go no further. The Marines killed the 150 to 200 Japs who fought to the last. Three officers and twenty-six men of the battalion were killed, and about six officers and sixty men were wounded. On Abemama, the other Gilbert atoll where there were Japs, about thirty Marine scouts had landed and hemmed in the Japs. One Marine was killed; the twenty-five Japs committed suicide.

By now the LST's have nosed up to the edge of the shelf that surrounds Betio. At low tide they discharge trucks by the dozen which carry supplies ashore over the coral flats, through the hole that has been cut into the seawall. Within a very few days Betio will be a strong American base—stronger offensively than the Japs had made it defensively.

Not until next day did we learn that three Marines had been killed on the western end of the island by Jap snipers, shortly after the generals had passed that point.

On the sixth day I walked over the eastern half of Betio— the half which got almost as much attention prior to the landing as the western half, plus an additional four days' pounding by every gun in the U. S. Navy, every gun up to 75 mm. in the U. S. Marine Corps, and many hundreds of Navy bombers and fighters. If the western half was a shambles, the tail end was the acme of destruction and desolation. Shellholes and bomb craters, uprooted coconut trees, exploded ammunition dumps, some pulverized pillboxes, big guns broken and bent, and many hundreds of rotting Japanese bodies. This is the route I took in viewing the carnage on the tail end of Betio:

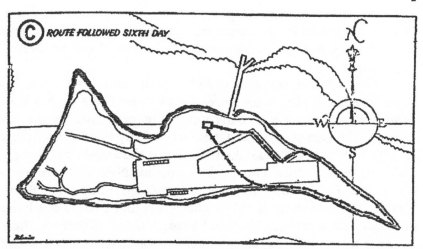

At the pillbox near Major Crowe's headquarters where I had seen the first Jap fried by a flamethrower, I note the details of the fortification, now that it has been stripped down by repeated charges of TNT. The three feet of sand that covered its rounded top has been blasted away. The top actually was a cone-shaped piece of armor, two layers of quarter-inch steel. Beneath that steel turret there were two layers of eight-inch coconut logs—the turret armor was used apparently to give the top a rounded shape which would deflect bombs. This pillbox was five-sided, each side about ten feet, with a buffer tier at the entrance for protection against shrapnel. Each side consisted of a double tier of coconut logs, hooked together by steel spikes with sand between the tiers. Over the whole, including the sides, there was a deep layer of sand, which gave the pillbox the appearance of a tropical igloo. There were two entrances to the pillbox—one to seaward and one to the east.

The machine-gun emplacements on the north side of the island's tail are much the same as those on the west end. Beside them and back of them there are trenches, some containing twenty-five Jap dead. Inland thirty yards there is a fifteen-foot-high cement-and-coconut-log, sand-covered ammunition dump. There are gashes in the coconut logs where the sand has been blasted away, but no penetration by hundreds of rounds of high explosives.

A mess kitchen, with two-by-four walls and a tin roof, has been blasted to bits. It measures about twenty-five by one-hundred feet and there are many ten-gallon pots laid on the fire holes in the cement stoves. A hen sets calmly inside the debris. At the east end of the kitchen there are thousands upon thousands of cans of food and broken bottles. Nearby there are a dozen half-Japs whose life had been flicked away by a flame-thrower. One of them is only a charred spinal cord and a lump of burnt flesh where his head had been. A little further on, there are fifty more dead Japs—they seem to be thicker on this end of the island. Scattered around a big blockhouse and what apparently had been a power plant there are at least 150 more who had been hit by a variety of weapons: some are charred, others have their heads blown off, others are only chests or trunks. Only one of them appears to be a suicide. In the midst of them there is a lone Marine, lying under two sprawling Japs. What had been this man's fate—this man whose pack containing two cans of C ration had been ripped by shrapnel? Had he been killed by a Jap bullet, or hit by some of our own high explosives? Or had he single-handed tried to attack 150 Japs? No reporter is ever likely to answer that question.

The march up the tail of the island is strewn with carnage. Now, on the sixth day, the smell of the dead is unbelievable. The ruptured and twisted bodies which expose their rotting inner organs are inexpressibly repelling. Betio would be more habitable if the Marines could leave for a few days and send a million buzzards in. The fire from a burning pile of rubble has reached six nearby Jap bodies, which sizzle and pop as the flame consumes flesh and gases. Fifteen more are scattered around a food dump, and two others are blown to a hundred pieces—a hand here, a head there, a hobnailed foot farther away.

There is a warehouse near the end of the Burns Philp pier, whose contents have been scattered over many hundreds of square feet. A small trolley leads from the end of the pier to the warehouse. Unlike the Jap Army on Attu, the Navy troops on Tarawa were well supplied with mechanized tools and vehicles. Next to the pier there is another armored turret that served atop a pillbox. This one is smashed in on two sides, and perforated a hundred times by strafing bullets. Two Japs are in a shellhole that was a coconut-log pillbox—here the additional four days of shelling proves that some of these pillboxes can be smashed by heavy gunfire. Under the Burns Philp pier lie a dozen Japs who machine-gunned the Americans as they waded ashore (a destroyer finally smashed the pier). Under a privy platform which is also smashed lie fourteen more Japs. At the end of this pier lies a pig, his hams shot off. Three wrecked barges are on the beach. Two of them have double-fuselaged bows, look something like P-38's.

Inland there is one of the biggest concrete blockhouses on the island—about sixty by forty, and twenty-five feet high. Four direct hits, probably from battleships, smashed through its walls, and a Marine souvenir-hunter says there are 300 charred Jap bodies inside. Steps lead to the roof of the blockhouse, where there are two 13-mm. machine guns. In one gun nest there are four dead Japs, in the other, two. Four others are scattered around the rooftop and two more are in a pen covered by sandbags. All apparently were killed by strafing planes, although some naval gun shrapnel nicked the extension of the walls which protect the roof-bound machine gunners. These nicks show that the entire thick concrete structure was laced with half-inch reinforcing steel. A Marine sits down on the roof, opens a can of C ration, and eats heartily.

Outside there are two burned Jap tanks, carrying license plates number 102 and 113 and the Navy anchor insignia. A black automobile in a nearby wooden garage has hardly been touched. None of the glass windows has been broken and there are only a few strafing bullets through the top of the car. An indifferent Marine gets in the car, steps on the starter. The engine runs like a sewing machine. Near the garage there is what was once a motor pool—the concrete blockhouse was undoubtedly a headquarters. A dozen motorcycles with sidecars are burned to steel skeletons, but one little motorcycle truck is in fairly good condition.

Another warehouse a hundred yards beyond is torn to pieces, but only one of the five coconut-log pillboxes surrounding it is not intact. Another warehouse was also the site of another motor pool. None of its trucks or motorcycles will run again!

Back on the north beach opposite the inland warehouses, there are three fifty-foot-long pillboxes and eight or ten smaller ones. One of the larger fortifications has its top blown completely off. The rest are untouched, but the mounted gun inside—37 mm. or 40 mm.—is twisted and broken, its wheels demolished. Further down the beach there are contiguous shellholes, and shellholes within shellholes, as far as the eye can see. A strong, small pillbox is smashed in, pinning a Jap machine gunner to the bottom of the dugout. The next pillbox also had an armored turret for a top, but it, too, is only a smashed steel cone.

Within a few hundred yards of the end of the island the Japs had used great bulbous roots of coconut trees for fortifications, back of layers of barbed wire and rows of mines on the beach. Back of the beach, where eight Japs lie in a blasted pillbox, there is a long tank trap fenced in on either side by barbed wire. A little Jap pack howitzer, about 75 mm., but having wheels only thirty inches in diameter, is the first of its kind I have seen on Betio. A 36-inch searchlight on the beach has been shattered. The coconut logs supporting it have been smashed to the ground and the machinery which operated the searchlight is good only for scrap iron.

Thirty yards inland from the searchlight there is another concrete blockhouse which was an ammunition dump serving the two nearby shattered twin-mount 5.5-inch guns. A direct hit on the ammunition dump had set off the shells inside, which blew the roof heaven knows where. There are hundreds of rounds of ammunition inside. The concrete walls are fairly well intact, however. These walls measure, by a twelve-inch shoe, just eight feet thick, which is a lot of concrete. There is evidence of only one Jap nearby: a leg and arms which probably matched. On the airfield to the west the first F6F lands on Betio.

Beside an unexploded five-hundred-pound bomb there is a hole caused by a bomb that was not a dud. Six Japs are in the hole, which is filled to a depth of two feet by seeping water. Inland there is another mess kitchen with a capacity for ten ten-gallon pots. Near it there had been a barracks building of which now only the floor remains. Scattered around the remains of the building are blankets, shoes, buttons, underwear, "writing pads" —so labeled in English, pans and cups carrying the Navy insignia, sake bottles. Much of the clothing is civilian—evidently there were quite a few Japanese civilians on Betio, or the Navy takes its civilian clothes with it. My souvenir of Betio is a fine, red-figured Japanese silk necktie.

Near the tail end of the island I cross the 150 yards to the southern shore. In the middle of the tail end of the island there are hundreds of tons of unrusted steel rail and at least a thousand wheels to fit those rails. Unmistakably, the Japs had big plans for Betio.

On the south shore, near the tail end, are the remains of two more eight-inch Vickers guns. One of the gun barrels is broken off about four feet from where it sticks out of the turret. The other gun is badly burned and strafing bullets had nicked the inside of the barrel so badly that it probably could not have been fired again. There are three searchlights within 300 yards, and numerous 13-mm. and 77-mm. anti-aircraft guns protect the big guns. Not far away there are twenty dead Japs in a shellhole. Perhaps they had worked at the mixer which had been pouring dozens of pyramidal concrete blocks for the defense of Betio against the expected American invasion.

By running most of the mile and a half back to the pier, past Seabees and trucks and graders and rollers working on the airfield, past several hundred more dead Japs and one well-hidden live Jap who pestered the Seabees, past hundreds of shellholes and bomb craters of varying depths, I made the plane for Funafuti. I was not sorry to leave the appalling wreckage of Betio and its 5,000 dead. I was thankful that I had lived through the toughest job ever assigned to the toughest outfit the U. S. has produced: the magnificent U. S. Marines.

That night as I gratefully soaped myself in an outdoor shower on Funafuti, Co-pilot Hugh Wilkinson said, "I hated to tell you this when you boarded the plane at Tarawa, but all of you smelled like dead Japs." Lieutenant Wilkinson gave me some of his clothing, for I had none except the dirty Marine dungarees I had worn for six days. "Can't I give you these in exchange?" I said. "Perhaps a native woman would wash them."

Said Wilkinson, "Thanks just the same, but I think we'll bury the dungarees. Let's go get a bottle of beer."

AFTERTHOUGHTS

Just EIGHT DAYS after the first Marines hit the beach at Betio, I was again in Honolulu. Already there were rumblings about Tarawa. People on the U. S. mainland had gasped when they heard the dread phrase, "heavy casualties." They gasped again when it was announced that 1,026 Marines had been killed, 2,600 wounded.* "This must not happen again," thundered an editorial. "Our intelligence must have been faulty," guessed a member of Congress.

This attitude, following the finest victory U. S. troops had won in this war, was amazing. It was the clearest indication that the peacetime United States (i.e., the United States as of December, 1943) simply found it impossible to bridge the great chasm that separates the pleasures of peace from the horrors of war. Like the generation they educated, the people had not thought of war in terms of men being killed—war seemed so far away.

Tarawa, it seemed to me, marked the beginning of offensive thrusts in the Pacific. Tarawa appeared to be the opening key

* This first estimate actually was somewhat higher than revised casualty figures: 685 killed, 77 died of wounds, 169 missing, about 2100 wounded.

to offensive operations throughout the whole Pacific—as important in its way as Guadalcanal was important to the defense of the U. S.-Australian supply line. Tarawa required four days; Guadalcanal, six months. Total casualties among Marines alone, not even including malaria cases, were about twenty percent higher on Guadalcanal.

Tarawa was not perfectly planned or perfectly executed. Few military operations are, particularly when the enemy is alert. Said Julian Smith: "We made mistakes, but you can't know it all the first time. We learned a lot which will benefit us in the future. And we made fewer mistakes than the Japs did." Tarawa was the first frontal assault on a heavily defended atoll. By all the rules concerning amphibious assaults, the Marines should have suffered far heavier casualties than the defenders. Yet, for every Marine who was killed more than four Japs died—four of the best troops the Emperor had. Looking at the defenses of Betio, it was no wonder our colonels could say: "With two battalions of Marines I could have held this island until hell froze over."

Tarawa must have given the Japanese General Staff something to think about.

The lessons of Tarawa were many. It is a shame that some very fine Americans had to pay for those lessons with their lives, but they gave their lives that others on other enemy beaches might live. On Tarawa we learned what our best weapons were, what weapons needed improving, what tactics could best be applied to other operations. We learned a great deal about the most effective methods of applying Naval gunfire and bombs to atolls. Our capacity to learn, after two years of war, had improved beyond measure. The same blind refusal to learn, which had characterized many of our operations early in the war, had almost disappeared. We were learning, and learning how to learn faster.

The facts were cruel, but inescapable: Probably no amount of shelling and bombing could obviate the necessity of sending in foot soldiers to finish the job. The corollary was this: there is no easy way to win the war; there is no panacea which will prevent men from getting killed. To me it seemed that to deprecate the Tarawa victory was almost to defame the memory of the gallant men who lost their lives achieving it.

Why, then, did so many Americans throw up their hands at the heavy losses on Tarawa? Why did they not realize that there would be many other bigger and bloodier Tarawas in the three or four years of Japanese war following the first Tarawa? After two years of observing the Japanese I had become convinced that they had only one strategy: to burrow into the ground as far and as securely as possible, waiting for the Americans to dig them out; then to hope that the Americans would grow sick of their own losses before completing the job. Result: a Japanese victory through negotiated peace. It seemed to me that those Americans who were horrified by Tarawa were playing into Japanese hands. It also seemed that there was no way to defeat the Japanese except by extermination.

Then I reasoned that many Americans had never been led to expect anything but an easy war. Through their own wishful thinking, bolstered by comfort-inspiring yarns from the war theatres, they had really believed that this place or that place could be "bombed out of the war." It seemed to many that machines alone would win the war for us, perhaps with the loss of only a few pilots, and close combat would not be necessary. As a matter of fact, by the end of 1943 our airplanes, after a poor start, had far outdistanced anything the Japanese could put in the air. We really did not worry particularly about Japanese airpower. If we could get close enough, we could gain air supremacy wherever we chose. But did that mean we could win the war by getting only a few pilots killed? It did not. Certainly, air supremacy was necessary. But airpower could not win the war alone. Despite airplanes and the best machines we could produce, the road to Tokyo would be lined with the grave of many a foot soldier. This came as a surprise to many people.

Cur information services had failed to impress the people
with the hard facts of war. Early in the war our communiqués
gave the impression that we were bowling over the enemy every
time our handful of bombers dropped a few pitiful tons from
30,000 feet. The stories accompanying the communiqués gave the
impression that any American could lick any twenty Japs. Later,
the communiqués became more matter-of-fact. But the communiqués, which made fairly dry reading, were rewritten by
press association reporters who waited for them back at rea:
headquarters. The stories almost invariably came out liberally
sprinkled with "smash" and "pound" and other "vivid" verbs.
These "vivid" verbs impressed the headline writers back in the
home office. They impressed the reading public which saw them
in tall type. But they sometimes did not impress the miserable,
bloody soldiers in the front lines where the action had taken
place. Gloomily observed a sergeant: "The war that is being
written in the newspapers must be a different war from the one
we see." Sometimes I thought I could see a whole generation
losing its faith in the press. One night a censor showed me four
different letters saying, in effect: "I wish we could give you the
story of this battle without the sugar-coating you see in the
newspapers."

Whose fault was this? Surely, there must have been some reason for tens of millions of people getting false impressions about
the war. Mostly, it was not the correspondents' fault. The stories
which gave false impressions were not usually the front-line
stories. But the front-line stories had to be sent back from the
front. They were printed somewhat later, usually on an inside
page. The stories which the soldiers thought deceived their people back home were the "flashes" of rewritten communiqués,
sent by reporters who were nowhere near the battle. These communiqué stories carrying "vivid" verbs were the stories that got
the big headlines. And the press association system willy-nilly
prevented these reporters from making any evaluation of the
news, from saying: "Does this actually mean anything, and if

it does, what does it mean in relation to the whole picture?" The speed with which the competing press associations had to send their dispatches did not contribute to the coolness of evaluation. By the time the radio announcers had read an additional lilt into the press association dispatches—it was no wonder that our soldiers spat in disgust.

Said a bomber pilot, after returning from the Pacific: "When I told my mother what the war was really like, and how long it was going to take, she sat down and cried. She didn't know we were just beginning to fight the Japs."

My third trip back to the United States since the war began was a let-down. I had imagined that everybody, after two years, would realize the seriousness of the war and the necessity of working as hard as possible toward ending it. But I found a nation wallowing in unprecedented prosperity. There was a steel strike going on, and a railroad strike was threatened. Men lobbying for special privilege swarmed around a Congress which appeared afraid to tax the people's new-found, inflationary wealth. Justice Byrnes cautioned a group of newsmen that we might expect a half million casualties within a few months—and got an editorial spanking for it. A "high military spokesman" generally identified as General Marshall said bitterly that labor strikes played into the hands of enemy propagandists. Labor leaders got furious at that. The truth was that many Americans were not prepared psychologically to accept the cruel facts of war.

The men on Tarawa would have known what the general and the justice meant. On Tarawa, late in 1943, there was a more realistic approach to the war than there was in the United States.

TARAWA'S CASUALTIES

Reported through January 26, 1944

U. S. MARINE CORPS

152

Jay, William R.
Perkins, Paul
Stroud, Herbert
Summers, Arthur B.
Swanson, Harold
Wharton, Robert H.

Technical Sergeant
Carlsen, Harry A.

Supply Sergeant
Warren, Page

Platoon Sergeant
Barker, Elmer C.
Dickens, Rowe W.
Gurley, Joe
Halstead, Murat
Nedbalec, Jerry
Norman, Basil, Jr.
Pate, Charles S.
Trotter, George E.
Wheeler, Leslie J.
Williams, Leonard E.

Staff Sergeant
Bayless, Joseph W.
Bordelon, William J.
Kroenung, Wesley L., Jr.
Snyder, John

Sergeant
Abbott, Myron L.
Atkins, James R.
Audette, Osea A.
Bowden, George W.
Bozarth, David B., Jr.
Brackeen, J. T.
Cole, Duane O.
Darby, Howard O.
Dimon, Emmett L.
Dougherty, Michael D.
Farris, Fred
Filicky, Frank S.
Flanary, Kermit C.
Fomby, Clifton E.
Gerst, James L.
Gibbons, William R.
Haisley, James R.
Hubert, James J.
Jellema, John B.

Johnson, Hugh W.
Johnson, Roy W.
Kidwell, Julius H.
Ledbetter, Emmet G.
Lee, Lendell
Lindquist, Everett S.
Loyall, Lawrence L.
Lyon, Clifford A.
Maine, James J.
Marble, Bernard A.
Marsh, Everett N.
Mauriello, Ugo
Mitchell, Clyde G.
Moore, Fae V.
Morgan, Francis A.
Morris, Jerome B.
Odom, Millard
Phelps, Ulysses S.
Phillips, Kenneth N.
Powell, Frank C.
Powless, Henry
Randall, Dwight W.
Reece, Criss
Reeser, George R.
Richter, Leroy R.
Roberts, Raymond O.
Roll, Ralph G.
Simpson, Edward L.
Simpson, Robert E.
Skinner, Morris W.
Smith, Kenneth L.
Snair, Carl, Jr.
Stoddard, Donald D.
Sutherland, Walter V.
Thorp, Vernon L.
Van Heck, Robert F.
Wells, Vernon S.
Wichardt, Vincent H.
Williamson, Wesley O.

Corporal
Abadie, John A.
Adams, Clay O.
Anderson, Vern M.
Andregg, Henry, Jr.
Barrows, Merle R.
Berg, Thomas J.
Birdsong, Jessie L.
Bowen, Clovis William
Bowie, Clovis Woodward
Brueckner, Norman L.

Bryan, James W.
Burill, Russell M.
Cabral, Frank R.
Cain, Thomas D., Jr.
Campbell, Arthur A.
Coatley, Elmer W.
Cole, Oscar H., Jr.
Condelario, Vincent R.
Cooper, Thomas H.
Critchley, Walter G.
DePreta, James J.
Ecker, Clinton J., Jr.
Ellis, Harold O.
Fitzpatrick, John J.
Gagne, Arthur F., Jr.
Garde, Sebastian B.
Gautreaux, Lawrence M.
Getz, Allen K.
Gleason, Robert B.
Goins, Marvin F.
Goldtrap, Claire E.
Gonsalves, Joseph R.
Gorenc, Joseph A.
Guerriero, Anthony G.
Haywood, William C.
Hirt, Gerald A.
Hogan, Jimmie D.
Holland, Paul J.
Hopping, Ernest F.
Jarmulowski, Stanley V.
Karlson, Donald A.
Lanning, Hazen B.
Lantz, John R.
Lee, Wilson R.
Luther, Hubert C.
Marshall, Edward
Marshall, Richard H.
Martin, Elmer L.
Martinez, John J.
Massey, Stanley E.
Mayer, Stephen J.
McCall, Quentin W.
McGrath, John J.
McNichol, John V.
Meadow, Wayne G.
Miller, Harold E.
Miller, Walter A.
O'Donnell, Morgan H.
Paluch, George A.
Paredes, Osbaldo R.
Patterson, David W.

Pellenito, Andrew
Percer, Walter T.
Phillips, John E.
Pinckard, George W.
Platt, Thomas F.
Rasmussen, Albert L.
Ribeiro, Arthur E.
Rigdon, Marvin R.
Robertson, Mark R.
Sands, William F.
Scisley, John Francis
Sherrod, James H.
Shockey, Warren R.
Simonetti, Joseph M.
Smith, Glen R.
Snapp, Raymond C.
Snipes, Neal E.
Snyder, Robert A.
Spence, John S.
Trantham, Jack
Tuhey, Raymond J.
Valdez, Charles T.
Vaughan, Welver C.
Walczewski, Edmund R.
Wallace, Fred C.
Wallace, Frederick L.
Walsh, Robert A.
Webb, Hester S.
Williamson, William L.

Private First Class
Ackerman, Henry R.
Adkins, Ray E.
Agnew, Robert H.
Alger, Theodore J.
Allen, Randolph
Anderson, Harold J.
Anderson, Truitt A.
Ard, Olan
Armstrong, Jarrel M.
Ary, Clarence K.
Athon, Frank L., Jr.
Atkins, George J.
Ault, James W.
Ault, Joseph E.
Bacon, Thomas C.
Bange, Oliver L.
Barden, John J.
Bauman, Benjamin G.
Baumbach, Elden R.
Bayens, John R.

Begin, William W.
Bemis, Robert E.
Benavides, Philip U.
Bennett, Nelson C.
Berg, Bert M.
Bishop, Edward E.
Bittick, Rova E., Jr.
Blackmon, Clarence E.
Bohne, Kenneth D.
Boschetti, Joseph F.
Braddock, Abraham S.
Brandenburg, William E.
Braun, Richard
Breithaupt, Marion W.
Brindley, Warren B.
Brock, Roland E.
Brown, Darwin H.
Brown, Duane McL.
Brozyna, Anthony
Buan, Norman A.
Burch, Harold R.
Burrows, Merrill G.
Byrd, Harry E.
Byrnes, Bernard J.
Campbell, Douglas K.
Campbell, Floyd E.
Campbell, Lewis A.
Cancilla, Nicholas J.
Cantrell, Charles L.
Carney, Russell L.
Carstensen, Robert H.
Cashion, Marvin P.
Casto, William M.
Cavin, William F.
Charpilloz, Lyle E.
Cherry, Ray L.
Childress, Frank E.
Collins, Sidney E.
Conley, Allen N.
Conner, George M.
Coons, Sigal E.
Coots, Patrick J.
Cope, Benjamin A.
Courtleigh, Richard W.
Cox, Gene W.
Cox, Noah A.
Crislip, Franklin R.
Cromer, Ernest E.
Cullars, Willie D.
Currier, Charles B.
Cywinski, Raymond P.

Daley, Allan C.
Daman, Victor M.
Daniels, Aaron
De Lellis, John C.
Deauchamp, Frederick J.
Dehring, Roger W.
Dekker, Howard R.
Despierto, Andrew E.
Drucker, Maurice J.
Drumheiser, Clarence E.
Duff, Harris K.
Duffy, John E.
Dull, Raymond O.
Eckhardt, Kenneth F.
Edwards, Alfred
Edwards, Henry O.
Elliott, Samuel B.
Fahy, John M.
Farat, Walter J.
Faria, Louis
Farino, Dominic A.
Fazekas, Ernest A.
Feeney, John T.
Fein, Bernard J.
Feldner, Victor H.
Feltmeier, William C.
Fish, William L.
Ford, Donald R.
Fox, Jack, Jr.
Fox, Robert W.
Funk, Oliver A.
Galland, Mervin D.
Gamble, James H.
Gambrell, Donnell E.
Garrison, Lawrence E.
Gaviglia, Victor J.
Gehrig, John C.
Gillen, John E.
Gillis, Basil J.
Gilman, Paul D.
Glowacz, Stanley S.
Goff, Ralph V.
Gore, Ben H.
Gow, Morris S.
Grant, Charles R.
Green, Michael
Greer, John C., Jr.
Griffon, Joseph
Hancock, J. L.
Hannon, Harold P.
Harris, Jay C.

Harrison, Arnold, Jr.
Harrison, Jess R., Jr.
Hatch, Robert J.
Hayden, Harold W.
Headley, Chester J.
Hedger, Reuben E.
Hein, Frank
Hein, James L.
Hensel, George R.
Herbig, Theodore R.
Herman, Bob D.
Hill, Jack E.
Hoffman, John W., Jr.
Holm, John W.
Holt, Clifford
Hoskin, Donald F.
Hullinger, William V.
Hunter, Donald F.
Hutchison, Orville A.
Hyde, Preston F.
Ice, Robert L.
James, Ernest C.
James, Ray
Jarrett, Russell L.
Jeffries, Thomas E.
Jenkins, Robert M.
Jenks, Robert D.
Johnson, Andrew D.
Johnson, James B.
Johnson, Robert S.
Johnson, Thomas F.
Johnston, Robert E.
Jones, Cecil R.
Jorgensen, Herbert O.
Jorgensen, Wesley P.
Katsulis, Demosthenes V.
Kellner, Frank J.
Knowles, Clifford L.
Kocopy, Michael
Kountzman, Ralph C.
Kourkos, Sam J.
Krchmar, Frank V.
Krieger, Jack H.
Kristal, Leonard E.
Kroll, William A.
Krzys, Marcel J.
Kubarski, Chester J.
Kuykendall, Elias
Lam, Francis P.
Langan, John P.
Larson, Oscar B.

Latin, Joseph A.
Law, John A., Jr.
Lawick, Walter J.
Lawrence, Robert J.
Lawson, Gordon K.
Le Roy, Hartley S.
Lee, Raymond N.
Lee, Robert E.
Leland, James G.
Lemay, Sylvio
Lemberg, Walter A.
Leveridge, Seldon
Lewis, Kenneth I.
Light, Joseph T.
Likens, Kenneth W.
Liles, Doyne A.
Lillie, Frank R.
Limburg, William H.
Limpach, Cleatis U.
Livermore, Joseph R.
Lorenz, Henry
Luedtke, Daryl M.
Lundrigan, Carol E.
Lutzow, Henry
MacDonald, John W.
Mahaffey, Robert L.
Maidment, Roger V.
Mang, Jack W.
Mannise, Joseph J.
Mannix, Kenneth F.
Mansfield, James F.
Markey, John J., Jr.
Mathewson, Harold G.
Mathies, Elmer L., Jr.
Mattern, Wilbur C.
Mayer, Milton J.
McDermott, Giles, Jr.
McDonald, Ambrose A.
McDowell, William J.
McGhee, Cecil E.
McIalwain, Stanley L.
McKay, William S.
McManus, Michael A.
McNeil, Ralph C.
Menendez, Manuel
Menger, Arthur G.
Meyers, William J.
Mickelsen, James G.
Miller, Charles D.
Miller, Gordon P.
Miller, Jack E.

Miller, Walter J.
Millick, Arnold R.
Minick, Zihlman T.
Monick, Francis J.
Montague, Charles
Moore, Ned L.
Moran, William E.
Motz, Robert L.
Murray, George B.
Nalazek, Edward A.
Nicar, William R.
Nunes, Manuel, Jr.
O'Boyle, Anthony A.
O'Hair, Robert W.
Oetjen, Charles E.
Olano, Philip L.
Olson, Oscar L.
Osmanski, Eugene
Osterman, Budd A.
Otto, Norbert O.
Palmira, Dominic A.
Parsons, Samuel R.
Paulson, Ralph L.
Pegg, Elzieathin A.
Peralta, Ernest P.
Perkins, Harold E.
Philippe, Robert S.
Philips, Cleo M.
Pickering, Raymond A.
Pilgrim, Luther W.
Poeta, John G.
Polich, George A.
Polmaskitch, Andrew, Jr.
Powell, Glenn E.
Prince, Forrest B.
Prince, John F.
Racener, Joe D.
Ragsdale, Howard E.
Redmann, Gregory
Reeder, Otto
Reilly, James P.
Reynolds, John D.
Reynolds, Marvin T.
Rice, James F.
Riggin, James M.
Robbins, Gilbert E.
Robert, Marion P.
Roberts, Larry R.
Rodriguez, Jorge I.
Romancik, Raymond J
Rommel, Max

Ruff, Thomas F.
Ruggiero, Eugene V.
Russell, Fernand J.
Russom, A. P.
Saini, John
Sanders, James C.
Sanders, Robert L.
Schaede, Roland E.
Scheel, Lloyd P.
Schempf, Harold
Schwartz, Marvin S.
Seng, Gene G., Jr.
Sentelle, Ottie B.
Shafer, William R.
Sheppard, Roy L.
Smith, Everett E.
Smith, Robert N.
Soeters, William H.
Somes, Arthur D.
Stark, Albert K.
Stephens, Raymond M.
Stephenson, Elzie B.
Steward, Richard M.
Strzelecki, Lee W.
Stubbs, Arthur R.
Stuhldreier, John R.
Surber, Christopher O.
Svoboda, Jerry F.
Sweeney, Charles H.
Taylor, Roy B.
Taylor, William F.
Thielen, Henry M.
Thomas, Harold V.
Thompson, Robert H.
Toros, Arthur D.
Traver, George H.
Traversie, Vincent E.
Trotter, Christopher W.
Trout, Glen H.
Turl, David W.
Van Zandt, Jack B.
Vance, Joseph L.
Vosmer, Ronald W.
Wales, Lafey L.
Wallace, Charles E.
Waller, Alvin O.
Walton, Orson L.
Ward, Donald E.
Ward, Gene C.
Warnes, Richard C.
Warren, Raymond

Watkins, James E.
Welever, Clifford T.
Wende, Arthur E.
Westfall, John C., Jr.
Wetelainen, George H.
White, Glenn F.
Whitehurst, James O.
Wielgus, Leo J.
Wiesehan, Louis
Williams, Alvin R.
Williams, David M.
Williams, Ralph L.
Wills, John W.
Wingler, Paul D.
Winkley, Manley F.
Winnemucca, Stanley
Woolsey, Freeman C.
Wright, Edgar W.
Young, James R.
Young, Marvin E.
Young, Walter H.
Zimmerman, Sherman G.

Assistant Cook
Masoni, Frank L.

Field Music First Class
Franciskato, Robert E.
Hoy, David C.
Keele, Roy E.
Nelson, Warren G.

Private
Andrada, Donald J.
Baribeau, Robert J.
Barker, Lowell
Benson, Edwin F.
Bitzer, Herbert L.
Blevins, William F.
Bolthouse, John A., Jr.
Boylan, John A.
Brentnall, James H.
Brophy, William J.
Bryson, Alvin C.
Byrd, Faris G.
Carlson, Glen E.
Castle, James S., Jr.
Coble, Edward D.
Cowart, William F.
Cox, Harold L.
Cruz, Jacob

Davies, Abner W., Jr.
Davis, Benjamin F.
Davis, James A.
Dill, Elvis A.
Few, George W.
Fouts, Eugene D.
Fox, Robert W.
Freet, Fred E.
Gasser, Allen C.
Geddes, Dale R.
Glass, Richard M.
Godin, Roger W.
Gooch, Erda A.
Goraj, Stanley R.
Greenwalt, Thomas J.
Grey, Harry O.
Griffin, Robert J.
Griffith, Roy C.
Guyton, Ezra O.
Hanlin, Harry L., Jr.
Haraldson, Palmer S.
Harding, Warren E.
Harris, Walter E.
Hicks, Wilson W.
Hillard, Robert W.
Hirst, Howard
Holtzclaw, Otho W.
Hornsby, Nelson La V.
Huguet, Lester D.
Hunter, Norman O.
Jackson, Aaron F.
Jacob, John B.
Jenkins, Paul L.
Johnson, Hubert C.
Johnson, Martin R.
Jones, Maynard L., Jr.
Jordan, Edwin W.
Kams, Harold L.
Kees, Milton C.
Kerley, Dillard L.
Kiley, William G.
Kines, Emmett L.
Kriss, Frank C.
Kuck, Arthur G.
Lally, John F., Jr.
Larson, Wayne A.
Livingston, Lloyd L.
Long, Harvey I.
Lynn, Everett E.
Lyntton, Max, Jr.
McCraw, Paul K.

McKinney, Robert C.
Messier, Adelphis J.
Mikel, Lawrence N.
Miller, Harley E.
Miller, Howard E.
Mulligan, James W.
Munn, Thomas J.
Oliver, Norman C.
Osika, Joseph W.
Osterland, Herbert F.
Pahl, Eugene D.
Parker, Albert L.
Parks, William A., Jr.
Parsons, Veral F.
Patrick, George F.
Pendergrast, Vernon L.
Penna, Frank F.
Pero, Edward R.
Pierce, Glen B.
Ragucci, Emil F.
Rambo, William E.
Redman, Jack M.
Reeves, Walter O.
Richardson, Glenn, Jr.
Roads, Addison B.
Salisbury, Harlowe D.
Salpietro, Matthew E.
Sharp, Arvil R.
Slobodnik, Andrew L.
Smith, Floyd R.
Smith, Robert L., Jr.
Spayd, Donald S.
Stambaugh, Jack R.
Stevens, Willis G.
Sturges, Forrest R.
Teter, Fay G.
Thomas, Edwin E.
Tillman, John M.
Tremmel, John O., Jr.
Tucker, Ernest E.
Tye, Harry D.
Vancil, Edwin H.
Varnado, Joseph W.
Voorheis, Donald D.
Waltz, Merlin W.
Wappel, Frank A.
Wetherington, Woodrow W.
Whately, Robert L.
Whitaker, Channing R.
Whitworth, James A.
Wilson, John A.

Wilson, Raymond P.
Winkler, Clifford A.
Wright, Richard G.
Yarbrough, James B.
Zazzetti, Joseph T.

DIED OF WOUNDS

Captain
Brown, Kenneth L.
Palopoli, Orlando A.

First Lieutenant
Hawkins, William D.
Leidel, Hugh D.
McNeil, Charles L.
Morehead, George
Price, Joseph D.

Second Lieutenant
Olson, Walter J.

First Sergeant
Quinn, David H.

Platoon Sergeant
Clark, Wallace J., Jr.

Staff Sergeant
Hamm, Robert B.

Sergeant
Brown, Shirley M.
Lowe, Clarence D.
Mahoney, John W.
Maples, James, Jr.
McGuire, Charles G.
Twedell, Donald R.
Veeck, William E.
Walker, Carroll F.

Corporal
Azerolo, Albert F.
Brown, Walter E.
Cecchini, Fred S.
Chappell, Wallace J.
Hodgson, Clarence S.
Hopp, Carl, Jr.
Lowery, Curtis V.
Martinez, Lester T.
McKibben, William D.
Olson, George V.
Wells, Winston

Private First Class
  Altmann, Theodore, Jr.
  Andervich, Edward F.
  Benson, James D.
  Blevins, Paul L.
  Browning, Homer B.
  Buchanan, Hullen D.
  Carli, William J., Jr.
  Chacon, George
  Chodl, Frank T.
  De Bretagne, Hugo J.
  De Marsche, James L.
  Foreman, John F.
  Frederick, Warren R.
  Gerringer, LeRoy R.
  Gibo, John
  Gilbert, William R.
  Gunter, Elbert K.
  Higuera, Robert A.
  Jansen, Joseph M.
  Jarrett, Afton H.
  Jordan, Howard K.
  Lewis, Ivor J., Jr.
  Lind, George H.
  Marcellus, Kenneth W.
  McPhee, Eugene M.
  Mohrlang, John K.
  Monroe, Thomas A.
  Nail, Jesse E., Jr.
  Norris, Joseph Maylon
  Price, Theron E.
  Rioux, Normand D.
  Silfies, Lester P.
  Soyak, Joseph M., Jr.
  Stebner, William F.
  Sullivan, Harold J.
  Taylor, Edwin C.
  Thaxton, J. D.
  Trimble, Willis W.
  Via, William D.
  Wallace, Charles E.
  ·Wickstrom, Carl A.
  Williams, Norman

Private
  Campbell, James P.
  Hill, Otha
  Mulroney, Thomas L.
  Pietrosilli, Antonio J.
  Roe, Milford

Master Gunnery Sergeant
  Dumais, Alphonse

Gunnery Sergeant
  Happe, Glenn

Platoon Sergeant
  Reynolds, Dornie B.
  Siwak, Eugene

Staff Sergeant
  Kovis, Donald S.
  Lusche, Carroll G.

Sergeant
  Cannaday, Herbert L.
  Del Bene, Paul A.
  Ferrara, Joseph A.
  Grimm, Elden W.
  Hammett, Harold
  Knodel, Reuben J.
  La France, Frederick
  Rasmussen, Gordon B.
  Yokom, Elmore F.

Corporal
  Barker, Raymond A.
  Beck, Milton M.
  Brand, Robert J.
  Bryant, Howard L.
  Clemons, James H.
  Gill, John W.
  Kinney, Curtis W.
  Krotow, Alexander
  Lane, Lambert
  Leffell, Hylbert
  Magehan, Harold C.
  Peck, Hubert A.
  Scheidt, George J.
  Swigert, Robert
  Vollmer, Daniel L.
  Watson, William R.
  Way, Herman L.

Private First Class
  Belter, Clarence B.
  Benvenuto, Francisco
  Brown, Marcus
  Burke, John T.

Calvin, Raymond D.
Cronkhite, Harry
Doss, Phillip I.
Emond, Lawrence G.
Facchiano, Alfred J.
Fedorski, Gregory J.
Garrity, Paul R.
Geczy, Joseph E.
Getson, Matthew, Jr.
Graeser, Stanley S.
Graves, Willis R.
Hamilton, Pembroke T.
Harris, Thomas R.
Harry, Billy, Jr.
Hudson, Ralph L.
Hull, Jerold R.
Johns, James E.
Johnson, Edgar R.
Johnson, Robert C.
Jones, Walter H.
Kaput, Chester W.
Kegley, Ellis
Kimball, Rolland E.
Kneff, James C.
Krenkle, Philip H.
Laycock, Morris B.
Liertz, Robert E.
Lower, Quincy McW.
Lukie, Joe
Madonia, Andrea J.
McCoy, Cecil R.
Mendes, Alvaro C.
Molles, Jeoze C.
Moreau, Braxton I.
Newman, Kenneth F.
Nickey, Robert A.
Norton, Thomas J.
Osmers, John H.
Ouellette, Fernand L.
Overman, Norman C.
Paulauski, Edward R.
Peters, Wyman L.
Pfeffer, Robert G.
Rawlins, Joe H.
Riser, Merton R.
Rivet, Ray A.
Ross, Lewis E.
Salerno, Michael L.
Sams, William R.
Sargent, Perley W.
Sauers, Myrl M.

Sazanovich, J.
Schertz, Paul E.
Schuldt, Roy I.
Scurlock, Thomas L.
Silver, Victor H.
Stewart, Robert V.
Strange, Albert
Sutherland, Frank C.
Templeton, Jay R.
Thompson, Leonard A.
Tolson, Donald R.
Tyma, Leonard A.
Van Engen, Louis J.
Ver Vaecke, Camille T.
Waldenville, Arthur B.
Walker, Charles D.
Waterman, Francis E.
Wiley, Robert
Wilson, Howard D.
Wininger, Rondal E.
Winters, Rondus T.
Wise, Philip G.
Young, Laurence D.
Zrolke, George

Private
Andruseasky, Frank C.
Avant, Owen C.
Barnhouse, Hamilton E.
Blanchette, Alberic M.
Button, Marvin D.
Carbone, Joseph C.
Carter, Broward L.
Cetrone, Peter J.
Chudej, Marvin G.
Coloske, Robert E.
Creech, John J., Jr.
Donaldson, William C.
Drew, Charles A.
Dyson, James R.
Entwisle, Ennis M.
Gandara, Humbert W.
Harcus, David R.
Harris, Warren C.
Heffron, Edward J.
Lazzari, Donald C.
Mostek, Raymond
Naffe, Joseph J., Jr.
Newell, Archie W.
Plumlee, Hugh
Rout, Albert M.

Shelner, Norman R.
Siegel, Clifford
Smith, Loren A.
Stamey, Jack
Stewart, Donald R.
Sturmer, Herman F., Jr.
Vellucci, Angelo M.
Verhaalen, Henry C.
Vocila, Russell W.
Wetternach, Laurence K.
Williams, Varden A.
Zalut, Stanley

WOUNDED IN ACTION

Colonel
Shoup, David M.

Lieutenant Colonel
Swenceski, Alexander B.

Major
Chamberlin, William C.
Hays, Lawrence C.
Throneson, Harold K.

Captain
Anderson, Harry P.
Bartram, Vernon L.
Bray, William T.
Cason, Alan R.
Cook, Paul
Corbett, Scott S.
Hoffman, Carl W.
Karcher, William O.
Krueger, George D.
Le Blanc, Osborne K.
Morris, Warren
Munson, Stephen C.
Ronck, Wilfred A.
Spradley, Charles B.
Williams, Maxie R.

First Lieutenant
Berg; Newell T.
Black, Terrell B.
Bliss, Welles R.
Bollum, Robert H.
Bonk, Edward
Cooper, George F.

Davis, Stacy C.
Doyle, Philip J.
Edmonds, Aubrey K.
Fagan, Kenneth J.
Fincke, James R.
Friedman, Joseph W.
Hoppin, Henry P.
Kavanagh, James H., Jr.
Key, Sidney C.
Kuta, Stanley J.
Ladd, Dean
Marion, Raymond J.
Morrow, Frank T.
Norvik, Adolph W.
Nygren, Wallace E.
Palmer, Joseph B.
Reed, James C., Jr.
Sanders, William H.
Sanford, Wayne F.
Schulte, Joseph O. B.
Seeley, William L.
Sisul, Michael J.
Starr, Elmer L.
Stearns, Earl J. -- --
Tong, John J.
Traylor, Melvin A., Jr.
Van Alstyne, John E.
Weber, Lee R., Jr.
West, Corbin L.
Wilson, Leroy K.
Windham, Sidney R.

Second Lieutenant
Barr, Joseph J.
Cochrell, Albert B.
Cogdill, Willard G.
Collins, Frederick N.
Culp, Edgar M.
Day, Francis L.
Dixon, Gerald T.
Ferguson, Lawrence H.
Gage, Willard R.
Grein, Roscoe T.
Grove, Robert W.
Hall, Robert A.
Harford, Edward J.
Harvick, Loyd S.
Hester, Charles R.
Idle, William C.
Ivary, Toivo H.
Kern, George F.

Kowalchyk, John N.
Langness, Kenneth C.
Larsen, Leor B.
Lefebvre, Jules C.
Leggett, Howard M.
Linkiewicz, Casimir E.
Miller, Buster W.
Munkirs, Robert E.
Pinch, William E., Jr.
Poppe, Elery G.
Rountree, Warren T.
Schultz, Leonard L.
Vlach, Lawrence F.
Wysaski, Frank M.

Warrant Officer—MG
Hall, Perry T.
King, Alfred D.

Sergeant Major
Borsheim, Alfred J.
Woolsey, Clarence O.

First Sergeant
Gard, John O.
Lutes, Lewis W.
Milljour, Bernard F.
Osterhaus, Wessel W.
Vanderbeck, Jack L.
Varlie, Harry D., Jr.

Gunnery Sergeant
Avery, Harvey F.
Barnette, John D.
Cado, Joseph A.
Carlson, Oscar E.
Cimoch, Joseph
Dunkelberger, Harris B.
Fox, Ambrose F.
Garrett, Guyten W.
Hendricks, Hoy W.
Herrod, Ted B.
Hill, Dave, Jr.
Kellar, James R.
Lagana, Joseph A.
Matujec, James
Mau, Lowell H.
Nichols, Ray S.
Reber, Glades S.
Spear, Michael
Towsley, Guy V., Jr.

Van Buskirk, Robert H.
Wiborg, Gordon L.
Young, Leonard R.
Zulinski, Clemens S.

Technical Sergeant
Shaffer, Samuel
Wimer, Morris E.

Supply Sergeant
Wallen, Eugene G.

Platoon Sergeant
Bright, Murl
Forrester, Paul L.
Grommes, Bernard H.
Haycraft, Hugh C.
Holder, Frank M.
Homewood, Thomas V.
Hooker, Hurshall W.
Knoll, Raymond A.
McLarry, William V.
McNeil, Thomas R.
Myers, Jene T.
Pinckard, Earle B.
Redman, Bruce
Roberts, William W.
Robertson, Raymond H.
Senger, Donald W.
Soto, Arthur
Spence, George E.
Stock, Ray G.
Trinka, George
Vestal, Edmon R.
Watkins, Joseph V.
Woods, David
Woodward, Don L., Jr.

Staff Sergeant
Bensen, John F., Jr.
Goddard, Cecil L.
Harris, Jesse R.
Lent, Jack T.
Soekland, Roy D., Jr.
Wellington, Adna R.

Sergeant
Adams, Weldon Q.
Albers, Darrell B.
Alexander, Robert W.
Andrews, Eugene H.

Ashley, Roy E., Jr.
Bailey, Forrest D.
Bailey, William T.
Ball, Iddo W.
Ball, William D., Jr.
Bass, John C.
Bayer, Jim A.
Beers, Elden H.
Bell, Kenneth N.
Bernhardt, Webster W.
Blanke, Eugene J.
Blunck, Lawrence A.
Bossinas, Nick G.
Brown, Marcus R.
Bruton, Herman C.
Bush, Bernard M.
Butler, James W.
Campbell, John E.
Camplen, Carl L.
Caples, Jack
Casenave, Jack H.
Coleman, Alfred E.
Collins, Freddie B.
Cooper, William C.
Coryell, Carl E.
Crombach, Charles B.
Cunningham, Grover C.
Curry, Sidney
Dudley, Wendell P.
Dunn, James P.
Eckstrom, Leonard C.
Eichman, Harry W.
Emerson, Don S.
Enos, Thomas M.
Ewalt, Manley J.
Ewert, Earl B.
Ferretti, Elmo J.
Freeman, Jay C.
Gates, Grady R.
Gaudet, Marion H.
Gordon, Arthur G.
Green, Walter
Greenfield, Thaddeus E.
Grinstead, Lester H.
Grote, Harry Edwin
Hayes, Jack H.
Hermans, Theodore M.
Hill, Aubrey R.
Hill, Calvin L.
Hirata, Manuel H.
Hitt, Alvin L.

Holder, Thomas L.
Horton, Lee W.
Housley, John L.
Hoyt, William D., Jr.
Hughes, Robert W.
Hyde, William F.
Jenkins, John R.
Jordan, Elmer O.
Justice, Frank W.
Kay, Gilbert W.
Keel, Benjarman S.
Kelly, William M.
Klopcsik, Stephanus B.
Kovach, Andrew J.
Krueger, Bernard
Laurain, Joseph W.
Livingston, Gordon A.
Maddox, Clinton B.
Martin, Fred D.
Mathisen, Harry
McAllister, Sam W.
McKay, Leslie A.
McNeese, Edgar B.
McSwain, Louis C.
McVey, Clinton E.
Mein, Gerritt
Montgomery, John D.
Moon, Robert A.
Morgan, John H., Jr.
Morgan, Peter D.
Nichols, Glen D.
Norman, Artie M.
O'Connor, John M.
Odom, Valter A.
Orr, Robert B.
Osborn, Lynn H.
Ossignac, Joseph V.
Parks, Billy S.
Patrick, Evan W.
Patterson, Carl J.
Peterson, Robert W.
Pinske, Leroy L.
Poole, William R.
Price, Darwin L.
Pukatch, John, Jr.
Raines, Henry H.
Reece, Ike D.
Reeder, John L., Jr.
Reich, Fred P.
Renten, Michael, Jr.
Rivers, Matthew P.

Robinson, William
Rogal, William W.
Rogers, Earl A., Jr.
Rummel, Lyman B.
Sadler, Robert H.
Schneider, William F.
Schondel, Vincent P.
Selinsky, William J.
Sewell, Robert L.
Sharp, Herman L.
Sibert, Donald E.
Singleton, Richard D.
Smiley, William R.
Smith, Delbert D.
Smith, Elbert E.
Smith, Lawrence A.
Sorbet, Charles W.
Spiess, Bernard C.
Stansky, Maurice F.
Stover, Judson S.
Swift, Lowell J.
Tessier, Leon A.
Thor, August
Todd, Ralph M.
Toler, Robert C.
Trimble, Houston L.
Trimble, Wallace O.
Tucker, Lenard E.
Vance, Elmer T.
Ward, Odell M.
Whitaker, Robert E.
White, John M.
Wilhide, Robert F.
Williams, John P.
Wilson, Joe B.
Wyss, Raymond J.

Chief Cook
Britton, William D.
Lewis, Vernon E.
Muskett, Virgil D.
Robinson, Berlin

Corporal
Ackermann, Donald W.
Aguilar, John S.
A̶l̶l̶e̶n̶, Joe D.
    ᴛson, Everett P.
Arnold, Thomas J.
Babbitt, Robert E.
Baker, James M.

Barker, John C.
Bearden, Joseph L.
Beckwith, Bryon D.
Becnel, Julian J.
Beerbower, Robert L.
Belt, Harry T., Jr.
Benn, Fred D., Jr.
Berge, Allen M.
Bess, Charles C.
Black, William E.
Bolton, Pat W.
Bondy, Homer C.
Bonnin, Joseph M.
Bowen, Ray H.
Boyd, Billie
Boyd, Granville W.
Boyer, George J., Jr.
Breszee, William M.
Brock, Milden E.
Broker, Orville E.
Brown, Alvie C.
Browne, Jerry R.
Bultman, Carl J.
Buonopane, Michael W.
Burke, Phillip R.
Burns, Donald W.
Burton, Cecil J.
Bury, Glenn E.
Carrol, Edward F.
Casaday, Raymond E.
Christiansen, Martin A.
Christie, Howard G.
Clark, Kenneth W.
Clement, Robert F.
Close, Richard L.
Cochran, William W.
Cole, Criss
Cooper, Patrick H.
Corley, John K.
Cota, Henry J.
Cozzens, Louis J.
Crawford, Howard F.
Culpepper, Carlton M.
Dameron, Wesley G.
Davich, Steven T.
Davis, Robert T.
Davis, Robert V.
Dewey, Thornton G.
Dickey, Herman C.
Dixon, Ira LeG., Jr.
Dochniak, Leonard J.

Dray, Adrian W.
Duke, Henry M.
Dumont, George L.
Dykes, Joe B., Jr.
Eads, William H., Jr.
Ellis, Efford C.
Ellis, Henry E.
Ennis, John M.
Eranosian, Vahan
Erwin, Byron L.
Esposito, Nicholas C.
Ewing, George T.
Feltey, Raymond L.
Ferguson, Robert
Few, Charles E.
Fitzpatrick, John D.
Flatum, Earl E.
Flowers, James D.
Floyd, Eugene
Fore, Jet R., Jr.
Foster, Wells B.
Francis, Fred J.
Frankenstein, Mickey M.
Frieske, Albert M.
Fulmer, Herschel B.
Gallagher, John F.
Galuszka, John K.
Garcia, Manuel V.
Garvock, Malcolm W.
Geankoplis, Andrew G.
Gordon, Abe
Gordon, Morris R.
Gray, Earnest B.
Gremen, Jimmie T.
Griffith, James H.
Griggs, James M.
Grote, Frederick W.
Gzemski, Benjamin F.
Haar, George H.
Hallister, Harold A.
Harlan, Ellis V.
Harrison, Robert F.
Harvey, John L.
Heard, Robert E.
Hellums, Dwight
Hess, Wilford J.
Hilligoss, Ralph A.
Hoaglund, John L.
Hoffman, Marion Van B.
Howe, Gene R.
Hunt, Ernest W., Jr.

Husers, Albert, Jr.
Isenogle, Robert L.
Jakubiak, Albert B.
Jensen, Howard G.
Johnsmiller, Robert W.
Johnson, Raymon M.
Johnson, Wayne A.
Jones, David L.
Jones, Stanley W.
Judiscak, Michael A.
Kalkomey, Charlie F.
Kalmoe, Morris C.
Kane, Thomas J.
Kennedy, Juneious C.
Kernen, John F.
Kocjan, Edward J.
Koske, Herman C.
Kreiner, Carl V.
Kreuser, Marvin H.
Lamoreaux, Ray M.
Larouche, Charles R.
Larson, Donald L.
Larsson, Alfred J., Jr.
Lawton, Walter G.
Leatherman, Paul
Lemm, Elmer W.
Leseman, Dick M.
Linton, Gordon L.
Lockard, Jack S.
Lockwood, Desmond B.
Loughary, Donald J.
Lovelace, Norman B.
Lundahl, Earl E.
MacPherson, William R.
Macuga, Waclaw
Magnus, Carl E.
Martin, Charles H.
Martin, David C.
Mason, Morris D.
Mason, Robert H.
Maynard, Robert C.
McCarrick, Frederick E.
McChesney, Fred, Jr.
Menane, Frank W.
Meredith, Ralph G.
Meyers, Frederick W.
Miller, Patrick M.
Miller, Ralph S.
Mingea, Daniel W.
Mitchell, Arlyn K.
Mize, Grady B.

Modde, Francis J.
Moise, Norman S.
Monachino, Sam J.
Montalbano, Joseph F.
Moore, Atridge L.
Morris, James C.
Morris, James O.
Moyer, Wilson T.
Myers, Audrey
Myorski, Stephen M.
Nelson, Mack W.
Nicholson, John B.
Nicholson, Sydney J.
Nickerson, Edmund J.
Nielson, Roger K.
North, Hugh D.
Nourse, Edward O.
Olivier, Leonce
Orgeron, Warren A.
Otto, James D.
Otto, John C.
Outlaw, William L.
Palin, Clarence W.
Peck, James A.
Peck, Richard A.
Peckenpaugh, Edward W.
Pendergast, Dallas E.
Penn, Jesse B.
Perkins, Gerald O.
Perko, Felix J.
Pestinger, Richard J.
Petersen, Kenneth O.
Poe, Melton G.
Pooley, Paul
Powell, Delbert O.
Presley, William H.
Quicksall, Alton B.
Quinn, Edward F.
Ragland, John R.
Randall, Sidney M.
Randolph, Ralph A.
Raper, Laudell
Reagan, Louis V.
Rector, Glasco W.
Rider, Charles L.
Robinson, Malcolm L.
Rogers, Lemuel V.
Roh, Frank J.
Romeo, Angelo L.
Rosales, Charles
Ross, Edgar V., Jr.

Schlievert, Richard D.
Schultz, Henry H.
Sharp, Robert E.
Shriver, Claude W.
Skenandore, Harding J.
Slama, Raymond E.
Smith, Sidney P.
Snell, Donald M.
Snyder, Frank V.
Snyder, Milford J.
Snyder, Robert E.
Solano, Raul G.
Spillane, John J.
Staroscik, Leonard M.
Swarts, Daniel C.
Tallant, James W.
Taylor, Carl B.
Taylor, Donald L.
Taylor, James W.
Taylor, Melvin H.
Teel, Delbert C.
Tensler, Orville D.
Thompson, Howard J.
Thompson, James A.
Turner, James H.
Turner, Lester S.
Twedt, Russel K.
Underwood, Robert P.
Vacca, William J.
Ventresca, Anthony R.
Wallace, James A.
Ward, Bruce E.
Wernicki, E.
West, Henry, Jr.
Wiest, Ralph C.
Williams, George B.
Williams, James L.
Wilson, Charles E.
Wilson, Eugene F.
Wimberly, Norman E.
Winterbauer, Francis G.
Witowich, Michael
Wood, Clark, Jr.
Young, John Harland
Ziton, Edward C.

Field Cook
Richey, Virgil M.

Private First Class
Ackerman, Frederick E.

Adkins, Everett D.
Alfred, John
Allamon, Richard F.
Allman, Leonard Earl
Amico, Guy J.
Anderson, Clarence E.
Anderson, James R.
Anderson, John, Jr.
Andreassen, John P.
Andrews, James B.
Anthony, Walter H., Jr.
Appelt, Clinton G.
Applegate, Robert B.
Arciaga, Trini
Armato, John J.
Armstrong, Edward R.
Arnold, Harry G.
Arrats, Sam
Arthur, Amos C. L.
Ashcroft, Woodrow W.
Ashley, William E.
Aubrey, Chester M.
Auck, Benjamin
Austin, Alphonse A.
Azzarello, Anthony
Babo, Chester D.
Backus, Clarence M.
Bahl, Vernon C.
Baker, Alfred C.
Baker, Clarence
Ball, Buddy
Bandel, Arnold F.
Banwart, Russell G.
Barkowski, Edward L.
Barnes, Russell D.
Barney, Vay L.
Barr, Wayne W.
Bartkus, Charles E.
Bartraw, Robert C.
Bates, Carl T.
Battin, Bobbie P.
Batts, Aubine L., Jr.
Baum, Howard W.
Bay, Alvin G.
Beacher, Edward L.
Beadles, Rufus H.
Beale, Carl W.
Beasley, Lloyd L.
Beatty, Harold E.
Beauchamp, Cecil H.
Beaudoin, Winston A.

Beckmann, Du Wayne W.
Beechler, John E.
Beegle, James E.
Bell, James L.
Bencina, Rudolph P.
Benedict, Albert L., Jr.
Bennett, Aquilla R.
Bergeron, Harvey R.
Bernard, Howard R.
Berry, Raymond D.
Berry, Richard
Bertram, William E.
Besaw, Leonard
Best, Edgar L.
Bevan, Joseph G.
Bish, Don C.
Bishop, Jesse R.
Black, James J.
Blackstock, Wayne M.
Blake, Marion J.
Bloxham, Robert D.
Boersma, C.
Boettcher, Francis E.
Bolton, Aaron W.
Bolwin, Earl J.
Bomba, Julian W.
Bomboy, Robert C.
Bonner, Robert W.
Bonner, Ross, Jr.
Boone, Alvin E.
Boone, Eugene M.
Boren, Noble M.
Borowski, Walter S.
Borum, Harold K.
Bowden, Arvin J.
Bowes, George E.
Bowman, Jack E.
Bowman, Robert
Boyce, Harold L.
Bradford, Eli, Jr.
Branaman, William H.
Brandys, Roman A.
Brayton, Wayne N.
Breaux, Fabian G.
Brew, William A.
Brinkman, Walter G.
Brisher, Robert E.
Britt, Bert M.
Broadhurst, S.
Brogdon, James M.
Brooks, Donald E.

Brown, Charles E.
Brown, Earnest H.
Brown, Max
Browning, Carl
Bruzelius, James A.
Buchanan, Harry W.
Buchholz, Carl R.
Buckley, Neil H.
Buda, John
Bukiewicz, Louis R.
Bunce, Francis E.
Buntyn, Robert M.
Buongiorno, Nicholas R.
Burgh, George B.
Burkhead, Robert J.
Bush, James H.
Busha, William G.
Butler, Ralph G.
Butler, Raymond E.
Butterworth, Fred A.
Cain, Andrew T.
Calaway, William P.
Caley, Paul S.
Calkins, Ernest E.
Callahan, Robert J.
Callaway, Franklin L.
Callison, Billy R.
Cameron, Donald O.
Cameron, William M.
Campagna, Thomas J.
Campbell, Ore L.
Canterbury, Harold E.
Caramsalidis, James A.
Carlton, Harry W.
Carmody, Alfred J.
Carpenter, Claude L.
Carson, Thomas I., Jr.
Carter, Joseph P.
Cartner, Darryl W.
Catletti, Russell K.
Cavaluzzi, Michael L.
Caywood, Walter T.
Champlin, Charles E.
Charron, Ernest C.
Charvet, Charles M.
Chavez, Thomas R.
Cherry, Verlie R.
Chestnut, Walter R.
Childs, George H.
Chronister, Wallace W.
Clark, John W.

Clark, Richard W.
Claud, Thomas J.
Clay, Wayne W.
Clayton, Johnie, Jr.
Clemmer, Eugene L.
Clifford, Freddie T.
Clinton, Walter P.
Coffman, Henry M.
Collier, John D.
Colton, Joseph R.
Comacho, Joseph L.
Condron, Virgil L.
Connady, Myron E.
Connelly, David F.
Conners, Raymond A.
Conrad, Henry C.
Conway, David O.
Conway, Michael F.
Cook, Alvin C., Jr.
Coomes, Thomas H.
Cooper, Ernest O.
Core, Richard E.
Cornali, Delphi J.
Corson, Irvin
Costa, Anthony J.
Coulter, Robert N.
Courchaine, Roland A.
Crain, Issac B., Jr.
Crawley, William D.
Crea, Frederick F.
Crook, Clifford T.
Crossan, Peter J.
Crumpacker, William E.
Crupi, Anthony, Jr.
Cruz, Pablo
Cunningham, James W.
Curtis, Earle W.
Cust, William C., Jr.
D'Agosto, Alphonso T.
Dale, Roy E.
Daniel, Theodore R.
Daniels, Preston J.
Darnell, James A.
Davenport, Roy E.
Davies, Bill E.
Davis, Edwin J.
Davis, James F., Jr.
Davis, James T.
Davis, John E., Jr.
Davis, Robert D.
De Coste, Arthur H.

De Hoet, Guy J.
De Jong, John T.
De Jong, Raymond L.
De Vilbiss, Kenneth G.
De Ville, Harold A.
Deane, George J.
DeLile, Normand A.
DeLucca, Ross
Denczi, George E., Jr.
Dent, Welborn W.
Derain, Robert P.
Derian, Albert V.
Desirello, Kenneth G.
Desmarais, John V.
Diaz, Henry, Jr.
Diaz, Raymond
Dickens, George M.
Dickerman, Jesse
Dickey, Dan C.
Diendorf, Albert L.
Dietz, Francis L.
Dietz, Howard H.
Dobey, Lawrence F.
Dobson, Claude W.
Dodd, Arthur E.
Dodge, William E.
Dowland, Gentry B.
Doyle, Richard E.
Duck, Carl E.
Dugas, Homer J.
Dunbar, Reginald H.
Duncan, Hubert L.
Duncan, Robert C.
Dunitz, Nicholas
Duplessis, Warren E.
Durbin, Forest H.
Durst, John E.
Dutra, John
Dwyer, Thomas E.
Dwyer, William A.
Dyer, Gamaliel
Earnest, Michael C., Jr.
Eaves, Coy J.
Edwards, James L.
Edwards, Rupert N.
Elam, Jack E.
Ellington, John H.
Elliott, Richard N.
Ellis, Francis W.
Engen, Harold C.
Eoff, Douglas D.

Erwin, William W.
Eschenbacher, Elmer L.
Essert, William R.
Evers, William W.
Faggard, Joseph W., Jr.
Fanning, Raymond A.
Farber, Arthur G., Jr.
Farkas, William J.
Farris, Arthur G.
Feck, Ralph
Fedor, Michael
Fenolio, Lawrence A.
Ferguson, Gilbert W.
Ferguson, James R.
Ferrick, Richard A.
Finitzo, John
Fiori, Joy V.
Fisher, B.
Fitch, Bill E.
Fitzgerald, Jerome T.
Flaherty, Robert M.
Flinn, John W.
Florentine, Dave J.
Flowers, Robert N.
Fluitt, Louis H.
Foreman, Alton
Foreman, Kenneth
Forren, Walter A.
Foster, John W.
Fox, George J.
Franco, Tony M.
Free, Roy E.
Frias, John C., Jr.
Friedl, Patrick G.
Froah, Robert L.
Fugett, Joseph D.
Gable, William C.
Gagnon, Henry J.
Gallagher, Charles R.
Gallagher, Patrick J.
Gardner, George W.
Garner, Seth T.
Garthright, Jack D.
Gasca, Lupe
Gass, Robert E.
Gaunt, Mark W.
Gawel, Louis J.
Geades, Harry
Gearey, William A.
Gebrian, Nicholas
Gee, Edwin B.

Gentry, James L.
Germain, Leonard M.
Giannini, Aldo J.
Gibbas, John P.
Gibson, James C.
Gibson, Mahlon W.
Gifford, Vernal C.
Gill, James F.
Gillis, Jay B.
Gilman, Albert B.
Glendenning, Charles D.
Goins, Amzy B.
Gonzalles, J.
Gooch, Luther
Gooch, Tommy R.
Graham, Roger M.
Gray, Dennis B.
Greaber, Michel W.
Green, John D.
Green, Walter D.
Gresk, Patrick J.
Gressley, Correll C.
Griffeth, Raymond W.
Grimard, Roland J.
Grisham, Leroy
Grotts, J. B., Jr.
Grover, Edward L.
Grumbley, George J.
Grzegorek, Michael J.
Grzeszak, Alfred E.
Guidry, Wilson L.
Guillen, Albert M.
Gunderson, Victor
Gustafson, Gilbert R.
Guthrie, Donald S.
Gutierrez, Robert A.
Gutowski, James F.
Hagedorn, Herbert C.
Hale, Bradley S.
Haller, Walter L.
Hamilton, Richard E.
Hamm, Gerald F.
Hampsten, Louis E.
Hansen, Erland F.
Hansen, Robert J.
Hardy, Kenneth
Harkness, Jack L.
Harn, Otis E.
Harris, James B.
Harris, Roy C., Jr.
Harrison, Ray T.

Hartley, Chad R.
Harwood, Alton M.
Hatch, Ernest B.
Haupt, James A.
Hauser, Frederick, Jr.
Hayden, Norman R.
Hayes, Harold H.
Haynes, Cephas S.
Healy, Patrick F.
Hearold, Walter M.
Heck, Robert P.
Hedderly, James W.
Heiser, Randell H.
Heldman, Charles F.
Henchman, John W.
Hendrick, Ray W.
Henney, Eugene H.
Henson, James W.
Hermann, Charles R.
Herzberg, Nobel W.
Hess, Herbert O.
Heuer, Louis M.
Hibbs, Franklin D.
Hicks, William R.
Hill, James R.
Hinch, Ewell L.
Hinderberger, Joseph E.
Hirschberger, Norman G.
Hish, Wayne E.
Hiter, James C.
Hoagland, Clarke L.
Hocking, Lyle E.
Hodges, Herbert J.
Hoffman, Reginald L.
Holden, George B.
Holecek, Edward L.
Holliday, Burnice
Holmes, John A., Jr.
Holmes, Sterling H.
Holt, Alonza W.
Hoover, Leland J.
Hope, Howard H.
Hopson, James R.
Horten, Adolph M.
Houston, Charles W.
Houtz, Ralph E.
Howard, Douglas H.
Howard, Joe E.
Howard, Joe W.
Howe, David N.
Howle, Marvin R.

Hoyt, Raymond A.
Hudson, James A.
Hughes, David T.
Huitt, Ollie E.
Humphries, Houston H.
Hunter, Daniel B.
Hurst, Robert L.
Hussey, William S.
Iassogna, Bernard A.
Iengo, Anthony F.
Jackson, Lester J.
Jackson, Lester L.
Jackson, Theodore P.
Jacobs, Billy M.
Jacobs, Donald J.
Jahraus, Merlin R.
Jaramillo, Henry C.
Jason, Clarence F.
Jaynes, Everett H.
Jazdzewski, Donald J.
Jeffcoat, Wallace L.
Jenkins, Percy J.
Jenkins, Walter E.
Jennings, Donald R.
Jessee, Edison, Jr.
Johnson, Albert E.
Johnson, Andrew W.
Johnson, Ben L., Jr.
Johnson, Chester S.
Johnson, Gordon L.
Johnson, Kenneth K.
Johnson, Mitchell C.
Johnson, Ramon F.
Johnson, Robert W.
Johnson, Russell C. R.
Johnson, Stanley D.
Johnson, Tommy L.
Johnston, Richard A.
Jones, Donald W.
Jones, George L.
Jones, Marvin O.
Jones, Paul B.
Jones, Ray
Jones, Tom, Jr.
Jostmeyer, Arthur A.
Judd, Rex H.
Kacin, Emil
Kaddatz, Wilbert A.
Kade, Frederick G.
Karalus, Donald H.
Katz, William

Kaufman, Kenneth L.
Kauzlarich, Charles J.
Kazmierski, Stanley
Keating, Herman A.
Keehn, Donald T.
Kegans, Cecil C.
Keller, William W.
Kelly, Roy A.
Kelly, Warren E.
Kelso, Edgar L.
Kemper, Leonard J.
Kennedy, Robert L.
Kerens, Thomas J.
Kessel, Joe L.
Key, King D.
Kidder, Leroy G.
Kiefer, Warren K.
Kimball, Lawrence C.
Kindred, Vernon W.
King, Robert G.
King, Vincent W.
Kirkpatrick, Robert K.
Kirkwood, William G.
Klein, Robert D.
Kline, Gordon L.
Kloepper, Vernon E.
Klose, Kenneth J.
Klosterman, Walter K.
Knapp, Edward J.
Knaub, William
Knox, George A.
Koci, Lowell H.
Kock, George E.
Koechig, Robert L.
Kohler, Gerald L.
Kokotovitch, John P.
Konruff, Ronald E.
Kopp, Frederick F.
Korupinski, William J.
Kowalczyk, Henry J.
Kranyak, John
Kreiling, Oren B.
Kubicek, Richard J.
Kulibert, Robert C.
La France, Robert L.
Lacey, Daniel T.
Lacy, David R.
Lambert, Ora D.
Lande, Kenneth N.
Lander, Robert H.
Lane, Francis E.

Lane, Leland E.
Larkin, Charles E.
Larsen, Richard M.
Launder, Willis R.
Lavrentiev, Nicholas, Jr.
Lawyer, James W.
Le Febvre, Roy W.
Le Jeune, Hillary J.
Le Penske, Donald J.
Lebret, Harry
Lee, John J.
Leffel, Dale E.
LeGrand, Charles D.
Lehman, Richard G.
Leininger, James L.
Lenhart, William P.
Lenord, Benjamin T.
Lesko, Frank A.
Leszczynski, Stephen P.
Lettman, James F.
Lewis, Alfred G.
Lilly, Charles W.
Lindgren, Leonard W.
Liput, Joseph H.
Lisker, Robert B.
Little, Thomas D.
Littlefield, Ralph H.
Lo Bianco, Joseph H.
Lockman, Richard J.
Long, Joseph U.
Long, Thomas S.
Longo, Raffaele
Lopez, Leonard
Lord, Clyde F.
Loudon, Donald H.
Lovejoy, Maurice R.
Lubic, Edward P.
Lucas, Charles F.
Lumen, Fred G.
Lund, Richard G.
Lupoli, Vito A.
Lynch, James J.
Lynch, William B.
Lynn, James J., Jr.
Lyon, Hamilton
Lyons, David B.
Lyons, Reeder F.
MacDonald, Robert N.
MacKey, Robert B.
Macaluso, Thomas M.
Mace, Delbert R.

Mack, John F.
Magnuson, Carl E.
Mahoney, Willard G.
Maisano, Clarence E.
Maks, Robert F.
Malia, William H.
Malone, James A.
Mangan, Michael J.
Manion, William E.
Mankey, Carl L.
Manley, Paul R.
Manning, Charles E.
Marant, Melvin G.
Marks, Lucian R.
Marone, Robert E.
Marriott, Jack F.
Marriott, William R.
Marshall, James G.
Marshall, Walter J.
Marsolo, Ettore J.
Martin, Charlie L.
Martin, Ernest E.
Martin, Francis C.
Martin, Ted H.
Martini, Albert
Matakiewicz, Michael M.
Mathiot, Earl E.
Mattei, Philip A.
Matzka, Ernest J.
Mauney, William J.
Maxcy, Paul E.
May, James M.
May, Oswell B.
Maynard, Richard A.
Mayo, Tommie G.
Mazurek, Arnold S.
McBride, Earl J.
McCafferty, Frank K.
McCallum, Willard E.
McCarty, Warren L.
McCauley, Brawley J.
McCleary, Joe P.
McComas, Bill
McCormick, Charles C.
McCormick, Kenneth D.
McCormick, Melba L.
McEwen, Albert R., Jr.
McFarland, Lee H.
McGee, Robert G.
McGillis, Patrick W.
McGinley, Jesse E.

McGovern, Michael J.
McGrew, John F.
McGuirt, Hazel B.
McHeffey, Winston A.
McIntosh, Robert B.
McIntyre, John P.
McKee, John M.
McKenna, James C.
McLaughlan, Patrick M.
McMaster, Thomas M.
McNally, William M.
McNamara, Robert V.
McNamee, Joseph G.
McNatt, Thomas O.
McPeters, Jack C.
Medeiros, Antone
Medvec, John, Jr.
Meetz, Victor G.
Melone, Anthony M.
Melvin, Jesse W.
Mendy, Joseph
Mercer, Charles R.
Merriett, Raymond S.
Mertz, Alton
Meuth, Bernard A.
Meyer, Eldon M.
Mickelson, Michael H.
Midgley, Robert H.
Miley, Earl M.
Milkie, Leo J., Jr.
Miller, Albert R.
Miller, Bob R.
Miller, Charles R.
Miller, Channing B.
Miller, Edward
·Miller, Harold K.
Miller, Julius H., Jr.
Miller, Norman E.
Miller, Swain D.
Miller, William H.
Mischke, Clarence J.
Mitchell, Billy J.
Mitchell, Charles W.
Mitchell, Joe D.
Montgomery, Joshua W.
Montgomery, William S.
Moon, James C.
Moon, Ray D.
Moore, Edward J.
Moore, Jimmie E.
Moore, Luther D.

Moore, Melvin J.
Moore, Paul D.
Moore, Terry C.
Moran, Kenneth E.
Moran, Robert J.
Moreland, Lloyd F.
Moreno, Eracelo D.
Morgan, Alfred
Morgan, Herbert
Morosan, Louis
Morrison, Eugene D.
Mottershead, Harry H.
Muggle, Kenneth C.
Murdock, Clifford M.
Murphy, Leonard J.
Murphy, Wilbur D.
Murray, James J.
Murray, Thomas E.
Mutchler, Thomas H.
Myers, Everett E.
Myers, Warren L.
Myrick, Orval K.
Narveson, Horace A.
Naumann, Russell E.
Neel, John R.
Neibaur, Mack W.
Nelson, David R.
Nelson, Robert G.
Nelson, Shelton R.
Ness, Daniel W.
Netreba, Nicholas
Neubauer, Leroy N.
Newbauer, Robert L.
Newell, Calvin L.
Newton, Donald G.
Nichols, Elisha L.
Niemczyk, Bernard R.
Nieminski, Chester J.
Nimtz, Verd W.
Nolan, Philip A.
Norman, Henry C., Jr.
Normand, Edward A.
Norton, Virgil C.
Nowaski, Kasmier T.
Nusbaum, Martin H.
Nutt, Darrell L.
O'Briant, L.
O'Connor, Paul L.
O'Malley, Patrick M.
O'Neill, James F.
Offringa, Richard, Jr.

Olechnowski, Frank
Olsen, Francis J.
Olsen, William H.
Olson, Donald W.
Olson, Lloyd L.
Olson, Melford C.
Olson, Varley E.
Orona, Tom L.
Orr, Daniel P.
Osborn, Carol E.
Ost, Eugene J.
Osterman, Bruce W.
Ostrowski, Arden O.
Otis, Robert A.
Otte, Richard B.
Pace, Angelo
Pace, Gentry M.
Paczkowski, Raymond S.
Pagan, George
Page, James N.
Paine, Robert P.
Panfil, John G.
Pankake, Warren B.
Paris, Ralph E.
Parker, George W., Jr.
Parker, Norman B.
Parm, David J.
Parr, Melvin J.
Parrish, Cecil J.
Parsley, Donald P.
Pasco, William F.
Paskash, Peter
Pasquin, Eugene J.
Patrick, Dean R.
Patterson, Orville L.
Patterson, William J.
Paula, Ruben
Paup, Marvin K., Jr.
Paxton, Joseph S.
Payne, Cecil H.
Payton, James G.
Pelkey, Bernard G.
Pelletier, Norman J.
Penfoid, George W.
Penland, Floyd M.
Pennington, Robert L.
Pentecost, Charles S.
Perdue, Jerry
Perham, Marshall R.
Perpich, Mike J.
Peters, James J.

Petty, Donald R.
Phillips, John M.
Phillips, Robert G.
Pierce, Franklin B.
Pierce, Tommy J.
Pinter, Theodore
Poderzay, Edward
Pollock, Harold, Jr.
Popaditch, Albert
Popielarz, Walter T.
Poppay, Frank, Jr.
Pottorff, Melvin C.
Potts, Lewis E.
Praught, Benet A.
Price, Billie F.
Price, George D., Jr.
Price, Richard
Proud, Richard A.
Pruett, Acil F.
Pruitt, Charles W.
Prunty, Lester L.
Pudelek, Chester A.
Pukall, Rolland W.
Pulis, William R., Jr.
Puro, Irving
Quealy, John M.
Radochonski, John C.
Radtke, Harlan C.
Redding, Charles S.
Reed, Joe E., Jr.
Reed, John M.
Reese, Warren J.
Reeves, Louis E.
Remmetter, Earl J.
Rendon, Edward
Rew, Richard R.
Reyburn, Wary H.
Rice, Russell A.
Richardson, Kenneth E.
Rightmer, William C.
Riley, Myrle E.
Rinas, Rudolph H.
Rister, Vernon H.
Ritter, Leonard B.
Ritter, Robert W.
Rivard, Jack H.
Rivetti, Vincent D.
Roach, Harold L.
Roach, William L.
Robbins, Marion G.
Roberson, Theodore M.

Roberts, Beauford J.
Roberts, John MacD.
Robertson, Angus J., Jr.
Robertson, Roy L.
Robin, George H.
Robinson, Warren G.
Robison, William H.
Roche, Maurice
Rogers, Dewey C.
Rommel, Jack
Roop, James R.
Rose, Harold L.
Roselle, Virgil E.
Rosen, Sol
Rowe, John T.
Rowland, Robert A.
Rozen, Edward J.
Runyon, John
Rush, Raymond R.
Rustin, Carl O.
Rutkowski, Joseph J.
Rutledge, Lewis R.
Ryan, Kenneth J.
Samels, Joseph D.
Sanford, Wellington D.
Sarraga, Andrew W.
Sarrero, Leonard I.
Sawyer, Donald
Says, Luther J., Jr.
Scheier, Joseph L.
Schenck, Walter P.
Scherer, Paul P., Jr.
Schersand, Cecil B.
Schiess, Charles E., Jr.
Schiller, Walter J.
Schmitt, Edward C.
Schneider, Lloyd C.
Schultz, Harry
Schumacher, Melvin C.
Schumacher, Vincent T.
Schwab, Jack
Schweer, Jacques L.
Scipior, Raymond A.
Scott, James, Jr.
Scott, Lyle L.
Seams, Lawrence H.
Seaton, Lealond E.
Sebastian, Albert D.
Seidel, Harry M.
Sessums, Jack W.
Severson, Gene P.

Shannon, Coyce K.
Shannon, Joseph J.
Sharkey, Jack
Sharpe, Billy E.
Sheehan, John F.
Sheeler, John B.
Shelquist, Harry, Jr.
Shelton, Gareld T.
Shinn, John B.
Shofe, Rolin J., Jr.
Shukait, Andrew A.
Siefert, Robert L.
Sikora, Henry L.
Silverberg, Morris D.
Simon, Robert G.
Sirotiak, Albert H.
Sirrs, Clarence E.
Sissom, Raymond F.
Slak, Frank V.
Slaven, John K., Jr.
Slinkey, Richard T.
Slominski, Harry L.
Smith, Charles J.
Smith, Eulis
Smith, George O.
Smith, Jack C.
Smith, James K.
Smith, James O.
Smith, James S.
Smith, Joseph A.
Smith, Manning J.
Smith, Robert C.
Smith, Wallace R.
Smith, William J.
Smith, William R.
Smollen, James F.
Snelson, Ottis L.
Snyder, Dean H.
Snyder, Robert H.
Solseth, Raymond H.
Southerton, Frank E.
Sovey, Frederick R.
Sowers, William L.
Soyak, William M.
Spagna, Francis L.
Spaman, Hollis G.
Spann, Charles E.
Sposato, Maurice A.
Sprey, Eugene G.
Springer, Ralph G.
Spurlock, Marvin L.

Sreboth, Roy A.
St. Clair, William J.
St. John, Homer J.
Stafford, J. B.
Stafford, Lyle E.
Starkey, James A.
Stauffer, John W.
Stavinoha, Edward A.
Steed, Ray R.
Steele, Roy L.
Stefko, Frank
Stegemoller, Ernst F.
Stein, Lee A.
Stenberg, Glen C.
Stephenson, Milton R.
Sterhan, Walter
Stevens, Carlisle P.
Stevens, Orville H.
Stickels, Berne T.
Stockstill, Billy J.
Stone, Clement W.
Stone, Robert A.
Stout, John R.
Strange, Adrian C.
Strate, Rex V.
Street, Norman A.
Stremlow, Eugene K.
Strickland, Leonard J.
Struckhoff, Eugene C.
Strycharz, John J.
Stulik, George J.
Summers, Velma U.
Suter, Raymond
Sutherland, Vinis H.
Swaney, Emory R.
Swaringen, Thomas T.
Sweem, Bill J.
Tasker, William P.
Taylor, Earl L.
Taylor, James H.
Taylor, Ray C.
Taylor, Robert L.
Taylor, Samuel M., Jr.
Terciak, Anthony V.
Terrill, Wilmer D.
Thomas, Edward A.
Thompson, James E.
Thompson, Lenard W.
Thore, George D.
Thorne, William S.
Thornton, Nelson E.

Tice, Robert F.
Timmer, Bernard J.
Tolson, Edward W.
Tonetti, Frank J.
Toth, Joseph W.
Townsend, Alvie C.
Trahan, Arthur P., Jr.
Trujillo, James L.
Tschida, Frank C.
Tucker, Joseph R., Jr.
Turbin, Jerome E.
Turner, Donald A.
Turner, Gordon H.
Tusing, Foster F.
Urbanik, Frank
Utz, Tommy H.
Vaccarezza, Eugene R.
Van Acker, Henry E.
Van Dover, Grover B.
Van Zant, Billy O.
Vanderpas, Charles W.
Vannest, Harry, Jr.
Varian, Homer A., Jr.
Varnado, Lawrence E.
Varucene, Joseph, Jr.
Veldman, Lyle E.
Verble, Claude J.
Versteeg, Wilbur F.
Villines, William H.
Vincent, James H.
Virgopia, John, Jr.
Voorheis, William H.
Voyles, Noah W.
Wade, Elbridge G.
Wagner, Norman O.
Waldorf, Ralph
Walker, Nolan J.
Walker, Richard R.
Wallace, Arlton K.
Wallace, William E.
Waltz, Royal L.
Warfield, Horace C.
Warta, Edmund L.
Wasson, Donald D.
Watchorn, Thomas C.
Watkins, Elwood
Watts, Carl Coy
Webb, Gerald Dee
Webb, Gerold R.
Weeks, Albert W.
Welch, Kenneth S.

Wells, Grover M.
Wells, William A.
Werling, Frank N.
Westbrook, Robert R.
Westerman, Charles B.
Whalen, William T.
White, Cecil F.
White, Patrick J.
White, Woodrow W.
Whitty, Edward C.
Whitworth, Milton
Wiedrich, Jacob P.
Wiesner, Abraham
Wiklacz, Joseph
Wilkus, Francis J.
Willard, Alvin M.
Willette, Jay R.
Williams, Clyde E.
Williams, Clyde R.
Williams, Don R.
Williams, Marshall E.
Williams, Newman E.
Williams, Wilburt
Wilson, Billy C.
Wilson, Chester
Wilson, Cullis R.
Wilson, Hobert D.
Wilson, Marion L.
Wilson, Robert L.
Wilson, Roy J.
Wilson, Wayne M.
Wilson, William H.
Wimer, Vernon G.
Windham, William K.
Wine, Kenneth R.
Wingfield, Lyndell C.
Wittkop, Joseph H.
Wojcison, Joseph R.
Wolfe, Thomas E.
Wolff, Homer D.
Wolfington, Garland R.
Wolpert, Joseph T.
Wood, Arthur P.
Wood, Ernest R.
Workman, Robert H.
Wright, James S.
Wuertz, William, Jr.
Wygal, William T.
Yancey, Joe B.
Yarber, Clarence F.
Yates, Cecil F.

Yates, James E.
Yehlen, Fredrick W.
Young, Robert T.
Zajac, Eugene J.
Zamora, Pantalion C.
Zaragoza, Manuel A.
Zaratkiewicz, Edwin A.
Zehetner, Robert L.
Zekl, Edward J.
Zglombicki, Carl J.
Ziegler, Otto R.
Zilinski, Steve
Zrudsky, Edward J.
Zuehlke, Robert W.
Zumer, Vincent D.
Zwiercan, Stanley J.

Assistant Cook
Durham, Royce E.
Zaborek, Henry W.

Field Music First Class
Bailey, Earl E.
Durboraw, Alvin B.
Foshee, Willie W.
Howard, Joe A.
Humphreys, Milford R.
Leavy, Donald J.
Wakefield, Edwin R.
Wholey, Joseph V.

Private
Acree, Johnny M.
Ahlin, Martin I.
Almand, James T.
Anderson, John R.
Anderson, Otis E.
Armentrout, Johnnie L.
Armstrong, Paul R.
Atchison, Marvin E.
Baird, Newman M.
Balducci, Thomas A.
Balmer, Robert M.
Balogh, Paul B.
Barbiere, August A.
Barefoot, Edward D.
Bartels, Vernon E.
Beach, Jack R.
Begay, Carlos
Begay, Charley S.
Begay, Jerry C.

Behar, Clyde J.
Benefiel, Donal R.
Berardi, Pasquale A.
Berchiolly, Samuel C.
Berent, Louis, B.
Bernhardt, Albert
Bernitt, Eldred W.
Berry, Frederick N.
Bianchi, Dominic A.
Bidwell, Morris A.
Blackford, Howard W.
Boehmer, Clifton H.
Bomia, Joseph G.
Bopp, Donald H.
Brodowski, Stanley H.
Brown, Fred
Brownell, Walter J.
Buchanan, William J.
Budnik, Donald H.
Burell, Howard L.
Burns, Clarence L., Jr.
Call, George F., Jr.
Cameron, Richard A.
Canavero, Edward F.
Canepa, Richard E.
Cannon, Bill
Cariello, Nickolas F.
Carmichael, Hardie L.
Carter, Robert, Jr.
Carver, Milton B.
Casaurang, Donald E.
Chapman, James E.
Christianson, Claus H.
Christilles, C.
Christo, Joseph S.
Cleveland, Orville W.
Close, Ferdinand L.
Coapman, Charles W.
Coffin, Robert
Coleman, Buford
Collister, Albert W.
Congoran, Gilbert M.
Cook, Andrew W.
Cooper, Junior L.
Coplen, Charles W.
Costello, Michael A.
Cowen, Stuart L.
Cox, Emanuel
Cox, Ovid E., Jr.
Curtis, Arthur W.
Dale, Harry R.

Davis, Howard T.
Dennis, Harry
Di Felice, John, Jr.
Doonan, William G.
Douge, Willis A.
Drysdale, Joseph F.
Duffey, James E.
Duitsman, John C.
Edwards, Joseph C.
Elardo, Sam F.
Eldred, Delbert H.
Elknation, Reuben A.
Elliott, Marion E.
Erickson, Eugene A.
Esler, Joseph H.
Feldon, Carl J.
Ferguson, Marvin D.
Fields, William E.
Finck, Joseph P.
Finley, Charles E.
Flaherty, Edward W.
Flaherty, Joseph B.
Flory, Stanley T.
Foust, William H.
Freeman, Cecil
Frost, Howard E.
Fryar, Donald E.
Fuqua, Kenneth
Garden, George A.
George, Emil
Gilley, Howard L.
Ginotti, Martin J.
Gladden, Luther I.
Glaser, Leroy W.
Graham, Taylor W.
Greenstein, Wallace J.
Grimmett, Rufus O.
Haas, Jack Leon
Haddock, Hal R.
Hall, Harvey J.
Haller, John J.
Ham, John E.
Hamley, Robert E.
Hamm, Clarence J.
Hande, Harry S.
Hanna, James F.
Hannigan, George A.
Hansen, Sidney J.
Hardy, Edwin R.
Harris, James C., Jr.
Harshman, Claude W.

Harwood, Milferd A.
Harwood, Victor G.
Hatch, Loman L.
Heath, Darrell W.
Hedrick, John M.
Heiman, Vernon L.
Hetherington, Wallace D.
Hicks, William J., Jr.
Hinderliter, Kyle C.
Hippauf, Gerhardt A.
Hlavacek, Leroy G.
Hoffpauir, Albert C.
Holmes, Harold A.
Hoose, Eugene W.
Horne, William R.
Hotchkiss, Charles A.
House, Robert W.
Housewright, Columbus V,
Houston, Clifford P.
Howes, Luther E.
Huffman, Paul F.
Huffman, Richard L.
Hughes, Hugh E.
Hunsacker, Robert J.
Irvine, John E.
Janik, Albert G.
Jay, Elzie C.
Jennings, Charlie R.
Jett, Harold
Johnson, Walter W.
Johnson, William A.
Jones, Clement D.
Jones, Estil
Jones, Jefferson D.
Jones, Robert W.
Justiss, David D.
Kent, Richard A.
Kerr, Richard P.
Kindt, William
King, Kenneth T.
Kloppenburg, Herbert G.
Klvana, Stanley J.
Knox, Frank R.
Korbel, George
Kovacs, Stephen J.
Kraft, Isaac E.
Kralik, Stephen D.
Kromer, Merle F.
Kuskowski, Edward P.
Kyle, John C., Jr.
L'Abbe, John L.

Lackey, Leo W.
Lagratta, Anthony J.
Lakomczyk, William J.
Lambert, Charles R.
Lambert, Gerald E.
Lanchett, Harry E.
Langenhan, Gunther G.
Laperuque, Clift N.
Larson, Richard G.
Lawes, Eugene H.
Leaderbrand, Jack E.
Leslie, Louis H., Jr.
Lewallen, Amos
Lewis, Dwight L.
Libby, Donald M.
Limnios, George
Lockwood, Roland S.
Loder, Walford G.
Lopez, Lupe
Lowell, Richard L.
Luccarelli, Vincent J.
Lutes, John A.
Mackrell, Alexander J.
Mannering, Wayne F.
Maresch, Leonard H.
Mastroni, Frank R.
Mathew, Jack A.
McBurnie, Edward J.
McCall, Donald E.
McCarthy, Gerald D.
McCausland, Walter P.
McClay, Burton F.
McGaff, George H.
McHenry, Charles E.
McLaughlin, Ira L.
McLaughlin, James C.
Meadows, George N.
Meadows, James I.
Meeker, Donald R.
Mehne, Fred D.
Menzel, Harold K.
Michi, Evo
Micklick, William J.
Mikkelson, Everett M.
Miller, Eugene P.
Miller, Roy L.
Minasian, Roy E.
Mitchell, Donald M.
Mitchell, William B.
Moldafsky, Harvey I.
Moore, Gerald R.

Morris, David F.
Morton, James E.
Moxon, Selmo, Jr.
Mrkvica, Louis J.
Mummaugh, Bernard J.
Needham, Gerald P.
Nelson, James W.
Nelson, Robert E.
Newell, Eugene F.
Nix, John D.
Niziolek, Walter V.
Nowicki, Henry L.
Nunn, Harvey M.
Oakley, William H.
Oates, Tommy N.
Oliver, Chester T.
Olson, Winsten V.
Olszewski, Steve
Paner, Elmer E.
Pernot, Charles W.
Pierre, George
Pinto, Robert B.
Pistono, Peter
Place, William E.
Pocialik, Michael T.
Porter, Claude H., Jr.
Przybylski, Melvin V.
Quinette, Thomas E.
Quinn, Roy E.
Ray, Marvin A.
Rayle, Ralph E.
Reed, Gerald N.
Reese, Edward O.
Reinier, Kenzie L.
Reitz, Harold H.
Rice, Heber E.
Riddle, Claude M.
Robenault, Russell S.
Roberts, Billy J.
Rock, Kenneth C.
Rogers, Dwayne E.
Romero, Ignacio E.
Romp, Lester F.
Rose, Roy Joseph G.
Ross, James D.
Ross, Robert W.
Saizan, Joseph M.
Salmon, Carroll L.
Sanyi, Joseph A.
Sarkisian, Harry M.
Scott, Gordon J.

Sedivec, William J.
Sell, Warren C.
Shaffer, Glenn S.
Shaughnessy, R.
Shawaryn, Eugene T.
Shea, Richard T.
Sheehan, Frank V.
Sheehan, Walter D.
Shelton, Weldon L.
Simon, Calvin R.
Singel, John
Sipes, Calvin R.
Slack, Harry D. T.
Smith, Frank J.
Smith, Hershel W.
Smith, James L.
Smith, Lloyd V.
Smith, Wesley F.
Sneider, Robert C.
Snyder, John G.
Soltys, Stanli
Sparks, Glenn W.
Spicer, Orville E.
Spickler, Darrell P.
Srock, Charles, Jr.
Starkey, Spates S.
Stauffer, Earl R.
Steciak, Casmier P.
Steele, William F.
Steinmetz, Kenneth G.
Stephens, Daniel F.
Stevens, Clifford R.
Stevenson, Paul R.
Stonehocker, Leland K.
Stoutenberg, Gilbert C.
Sturch, Elja E., Jr.
Swanger, Russell V.
Swindler, Lowell
Swoverland, Andrew M.
Tackaberry, Richard L.
Talbott, Russell S.
Taylor, Clyde
Taylor, John H.
Terlizzi, Francis J.
Thayer, Bruce I.
Thiel, Melvin H.
Thomas, Bernice L.
Thomas, Clifford L.
Thomas, Philip E.
Thomas, Robert E.
Thornhill, Francis L.

Tillman, Harold A.
Tollett, James R.
Trechell, Eugene
Trent, Jack
Tribble, Donald V.
Tuck, John Powell, III
Tuthill, James P., Jr.
Uhles, Russell J.
Underwood, Seth E.
Unger, Floyd D.
Uraitti, Lorenzo V.
Valentine, Henry M.
Van Horn, Donald E.
Vania, Paul J.
Vann, William I.
Vaughan, Harold C.
Velasquez, R.
Venus, Norbert R.
Vincent, William K.
Voigt, Arnold D.
Wagoner, James E.
Walker, Richard
Ward, Coy Joe
Watermann, Marvin W.
Weaver, Claude H.
Weaver, Robert L.

Webb, Marshal R.
Weir, Robert J.
Weisenburn, Gerald R.
Welton, Melvin R.
West, Eldon S., Jr.
Whitaker, Robert L.
Whittaker, George A.
Wiemken, Thomas D.
Williams, Rodger C.
Williamson, Jack N.
Wilson, James H.
Wilson, Leonard F.
Wood, Morris D.
Woolum, Joe D.
Wymer, Earl D.
Yoder, Charles D.
Young, Norman D.
Zbinden, Earl J.
Zimmerman, William F.
Zinn, Willis M.
Zolecki, Henry V.
Zuk, Paul
Zulawinski, Valentine F.

Field Music
Wilson, Oudrey

U. S. NAVY

KILLED IN ACTION

Vincent, Ward R.	Lt. (MC)
Welte, Edwin J.	Lt. (MC)
Anderson, Wyllys R.	PhM2C
Barker, James D.	PhM2C
Blancheri, William H.	PhM2C
Bowman, Joseph D.	PhM2C
Brisbane, Howard P.	PhM3C
Coburn, Henry C.	PhM1C
Cox, John R.	PhM3C
Gilmore, Raymond P.	PhM2C
Hale, "J" "A"	PhM3C
Hamar, Richard O.	PhM2C
Hanna, Robert G.	PhM2C
Hardy, John E.	PhM3C
Hildebrand, John K.	PhM1C
Kathan, Fred E.	PhM1C
McGuffin, William W.	PhM2C
Murphy, Thomas J.	PhM3C
Peebles, Kenneth N.	HA1C
Rix, Gilmore V.	PhM3C
Rogers, Ivan L.	HA2C
Shields, John W.	HA1C
Smith, Robert G.	PhM1C
Smith, Stanley S.	PhM3C
Talbot, Warren "A"	PhM2C
Watkins, Henry F.	HA1C

MISSING IN ACTION

Duncan, Merlin E.	PhM3C
Mareina, George E.	PhM3C
Skaggs, Hayward H., Jr.	HA1C

WOUNDED IN ACTION

Nelson, Donald R.	Lt. Comdr. (MC)
Bailey, Everett S.	HA1C

Blake, Riley N.	PhM3C	Porter, Paul H.	PhM2C
Brandes, Kenneth E.	PhM3C	Proctor, Wayne H.	PhM3C
Brookshire, Donald R.	HA1C	Redden, Malcolm L.	PhM3C
Campbell, Thomas T.	PhM3C	Robinson, Arthur	PhM2C
Carter, Lyle H.	PhM3C	Rodansky, Harold Y.	PhM2C
Crane, J. "N"	PhM2C	Rook, Kenneth H.	PhM3C
Divine, Arla J.	HA1C	Runyan, Lloyd A.	PhM3C
Dixon, Jim C.	PhM2C	Samora, Pete A.	PhM3C
Gunn, Joel E., Jr.	PhM2C	Samples, Charles E.	HA1C
Hansen, David E.	PhM3C	Schaffer, Melvin B.	PhM2C
Hawn, Charley W.	PhM2C	Scheinker, Harry S.	PhM2C
Hoatson, Clinton L.	PhM3C	Schmarr, Virgil A. O.	PhM3C
Holloway, George B.	PhM2C	Smith, George T., Jr.	HA2C
Hugo, Richard L.	PhM3C	Smith, Paul C.	PhM2C
Ingman, Paul H.	PhM3C	Snyder, John W.	PhM3C
Jones, John L.	PhM1C	Swift, Edward W.	PhM3C
King, Lester B.	HA1C	Tucker, Charles S.	PhM3C
Logan, Donald B.	PhM3C	Warthen, Vernon G.	PhM1C
Lusar, Vincent	PhM2C	Wedgwood, William G.	PhM3C
Lyles, Oscar L.	PhM3C	Wheeler, Arthur A.	PhM3C
Meyer, Jerome G.	PhM3C	Winters, Robert L.	HA2C
Newton, Earl E.	PhM3C	Wisse, Martin J.	PhM3C
Orin, Ervin L. D.	PhM2C	Wittern, William V.	PhM2C
Otterson, Marvin W.	PhM1C	Wodke, Robert J.	PhM3C
Overstreet, George W.	PhM3C		

Note: This list does not include an estimated fifty to one hundred Navy casualties not members of the Navy Medical Corps. These casualties were chiefly coxswains of landing boats and members of attached units such as air liaison and Naval gunnery liaison. The reason for this omission is that Navy casualty lists are not kept according to battles.

Nor does the list include some 700 Navy personnel missing after the sinking of the small carrier Liscome Bay. This occurred, not off Tarawa, but in the Makin operation.

Made in United States
North Haven, CT
25 November 2023

44538067R00118